THE BASIS OF THE PREMILLENNIAL FAITH

CHARLES C. RYRIE

LOIZEAUX BROTHERS

Neptune, New Jersey

FIRST EDITION, DECEMBER 1953
FIRST PAPERBACK EDITION, MARCH 1981
SECOND PRINTING, MAY 1983

ISBN 0-87213-741-4

PRINTED IN THE UNITED STATES OF AMERICA

This book is affectionately dedicated
to the memory of my grandfather
Charles Albert Caldwell (1863-1947)
by whose godly life and love
I have been greatly blessed

FOREWORD

Each succeeding generation must fight its doctrinal battles. As one of the last generation who has carried on extensively in writing in defense of the Truth, I greet with deep joy and appreciation the faithful and effective work of younger men on whom the burden must rest in days to come.

It has been my delight to read this discussion on "The Basis of the Premillennial Faith" written by one of my pupils, Charles Caldwell Ryrie. Here is sound Biblical doctrine presented in a most attractive way. The sophistries of men who pass over determining Scriptures without being influenced by them can hardly stand against such clear, exhaustive argument. Older men can release the pressure they have been under to shield the truth from the errors of those who claim to expound the truth of God when younger men assume the burden.

The essential facts respecting the premillennial faith are greatly misunderstood and often misstated by those who do not receive the direct, plain teaching of the Scriptures. For example, it is a common thing today to claim that the premillennial faith is something new in the world. On this and other points of misunderstanding, Dr. Ryrie has given a true and final word.

Considering the blessing that I have myself received from this thesis, I can do no less than urge others to read it most carefully.

LEWIS SPERRY CHAFER, D.D., Litt.D., Th.D.

PREFACE

Paul's question, "What hast thou that thou didst not receive?" somewhat expresses one's feelings upon completing a work like this, for all Biblical truth is a revelation from God through the ministry of the Holy Spirit to receptive minds and hearts. Then, one enters, and rightfully so, into the work of others as the history of doctrine is written. In a very special way, acknowledgment and thanks are gratefully given to the faculty of the Dallas Theological Seminary and Graduate School of Theology for their faithful ministry of teaching this student. *The Basis of the Premillennial Faith* was originally presented to them as a doctoral dissertation. It has been revised and is presented in this form with their kind permission. Acknowledgment is also made to authors and publishers whose works have contributed in one way or another to these pages.

Premillennialism is a system of Biblical truth. It is not merely an interpretation of one passage in the last book of the Bible. That the Lord's people may be informed and enlightened concerning this system is the purpose of this book. It was not written to stir up controversy, but it must and does state conviction.

May God, whom we love, serve, and for whose glory this was written, be pleased to bless His truth and exalt His Son in the life of each one who reads these pages.

CHARLES CALDWELL RYRIE

Alton, Illinois

TABLE OF CONTENTS

Chapter 1

Introduction

Last words of a parting friend are always full of meaning, and those of the Lord Jesus Christ are no exception. Shortly before He left this earth He said to His disciples, "I will come again," and these words have been the blessed hope of the Church through the years of the Lord's absence. Many Christians, however, have never understood the full import of these words, while others, having misunderstood, have foisted meaning into them. Nevertheless, in this consideration of the basis of the premillennial faith, there is no intention of merely adding to the quantity of controversial literature already in existence on the subject, but rather it is intended that the need for a thorough setting forth of premillennialism will be met in a positive manner. Furthermore, the intention is not to show that all premillennialists agree in every point of their system, for it is evident that they do not, and although differences and difficulties will not be dodged, it will be shown that they do not constitute major problems which invalidate the entire system. Indeed, the broad and basic outlines of the truth remain, and these form an unshakeable basis for the premillennial faith.

I. SYSTEMS OF INTERPRETATION

The word *millennium,* from the Latin words *mille* (thousand) and *annus* (year) is not found in the Bible although its

Greek equivalent, χίλια ἔτη, appears in Revelation 20:2 and 3. The word itself merely designates a period of time as such, but concerning the belief in that period of time which is called chiliasm, millenarianism, or premillenarianism there have arisen three principal systems of interpretation.

Premillennialism. In general the premillennial system may be characterized as follows. Premillennialists believe that theirs is the historic faith of the Church. Holding to a literal interpretation of the Scriptures, they believe that the promises made to Abraham and David are unconditional and have had or will have a literal fulfillment. In no sense have these promises made to Israel been abrogated or fulfilled by the Church, which is a distinct body in this age having promises and a destiny different from Israel's. At the close of this age, premillennialists believe that Christ will return for His Church, meeting her in the air (this is not the Second Coming of Christ), which event, called the rapture or translation, will usher in a seven-year period of tribulation on the earth. After this, the Lord will return to the earth (this is the Second Coming of Christ) to establish His kingdom on the earth for a thousand years, during which time the promises to Israel will be fulfilled.

Opponents of the premillennial system have attempted to obscure the main issues involved by inventing distinctions between historic premillennialists, pretribulationists, dispensationalists, and ultra-dispensationalists.[1] Such distinctions are not warranted since the differences involved are so minor and since the roots of premillennialism go far deeper.

Postmillennialism. This system, which took theological shape

[1] See Oswald T. Allis, *Prophecy and the Church,* pp. 6-15, and Floyd E. Hamilton, *The Basis of Millennial Faith,* pp. 21-30.

with the teachings of Daniel Whitby (1638-1726), teaches that the Second Coming of Christ will follow the thousand years of peace and righteousness. Though believing with the early Church that the kingdom would come at the Second Advent of Christ, Whitby stated that by the present gospel agencies every evil in the world would be corrected until Christ should have a spiritual reign for a thousand years after which period He would come to judge and to close the present order. A more recent postmillennialist, Augustus Hopkins Strong, says:

> The Scripture foretells a period, called in the language of prophecy "a thousand years," when Satan shall be restrained and the saints shall reign with Christ on the earth. A comparison of the passages bearing on this subject leads us to the conclusion that this millennial blessedness and dominion is prior to the Second Advent.[2]

Further, he defines the millennium as:

> . . . a period in the later days of the Church militant, when, under the special influence of the Holy Spirit, the spirit of the martyrs shall appear again, true religion be greatly quickened and revived, and the members of Christ's churches become so conscious of their strength in Christ that they shall, to an extent unknown before, triumph over the power of evil both within and without.[3]

The progress of evil has been so great in the past few decades that this theory has been brought into disrepute and generally is not held today even by amillennialists. The social gospel, however, has been an outgrowth of this system since the

[2] *Systematic Theology*, pp. 1010-1011.
[3] *Ibid.*, p. 1013.

idea of a world free from evil is envisioned as a result of man's efforts.

Amillennialism. One amillennialist's definition of this system is as follows:

> This is the teaching that the only visible coming of Christ to this earth which the Church is to expect will be for judgment and will be followed by the final state. It is anti-chiliastic or a-millennial, because it rejects the doctrine that there are to be two resurrections with an interval of a thousand years . . . between them.[4]

Amillennialism was born out of the theology of the Roman Catholic church which teaches that the church is the kingdom and therefore is reigning or should be reigning now. It had its origin in the teachings of Augustine who taught that the millennium is to be interpreted spiritually as fulfilled in the church. He held that the binding of Satan took place during the earthly ministry of Christ (Luke 10:18), that the first resurrection is the new birth of the believer (John 5:25), and that the millennium must correspond, therefore, to the interadventual period of the church age. Though he interpreted Revelation 20:1-6 as a recapitulation of the preceding chapters of the book, he understood the thousand years *literally.* However, since the Coming of the Lord did not occur at the end of the first millennium of the Christian era, amillennialists today hold that a thousand, a number of perfection or completion, is a symbolic reference to the complete period between the two Advents of Christ.

4 Allis, *op. cit.*, p. 2.

II. IMPORTANCE OF STUDYING PROPHECY

It would not seem out of order to set forth a few basic reasons for being interested in the study of prophetic themes and consequently for the existence of this book.

In relation to God. Christians should be interested in prophecy because of what God is. Either the world is out of God's control and His plan is nothing more than a patchwork quilt or He is absolutely sovereign and has a purpose and plan which He is carrying out (Isa. 46:11). Parts of that plan which have been fulfilled serve to demonstrate that He is the Truth, and thus that faith in prophecy is faith in God and in His plan.

In relation to the Scriptures. Fulfilled prophecy is one of the strongest proofs of the truth and accuracy of the Scriptures. That the prophecies which have been fulfilled would have been fulfilled by chance is outside the realm of probability. In addition, there is no escaping the responsibility of knowing and expounding the prophetic Scriptures since the servant of the Lord is appointed to declare the whole counsel of God (Acts 20:27). Sixteen books in the Old Testament and one-twentieth of the New Testament are prophetic, and one certainly cannot neglect such a large portion of the Word of God. Surely it is not God's purpose that any of His Word should be slighted; it must not be ours.

In relation to the believer. The study of prophecy will do a number of things for the believer. (1) It will keep him from false doctrines and false hopes. (2) It will help to make the unseen real and create within the believer's life the very atmosphere of heaven. One cannot do other than worship in reading the Revelation, for instance. (3) It will give joy in the midst of tribulation and affliction (2 Cor. 4:17). (4) It will increase one's loyalty to Christ and produce true, self-sacrificing service for Him. (5) When the believer fully realizes all the glory that is his future, it makes him satisfied to be nothing now. (6) Prophetic truth is the only thing which can give true comfort in the time of sorrow and bereavement (1 Thess. 4:13-18). (7) All Scripture is profitable and prophecy is no exception for it will produce and encourage holy living (1 John 3:3).

May the Holy Spirit forbid anyone who looks at these pages to be a hearer only of the prophetic Word, and may He increase in each the love of the appearing of our Lord Jesus Christ.

Chapter 2

Its Basis in
HISTORY

Premillennialism is the historic faith of the Church. To prove that statement is the purpose of this chapter.

Premillennialists are often confused by either one or both of two lines of attack which amillennialists make. Some, like Philip Mauro, deny entirely that there is any historical evidence of premillennial beliefs. He says:

> The history of Christian doctrine continues in an unbroken line from apostolic times to our day; and if it had been possible to produce from the copious writings of the "Church Fathers" any proof that the doctrine concerning the Kingdom of God taught by Scofield Bible and by certain Bible Schools of our day was ever held by Christians, real or nominal, in times past, it would have been produced long ago; seeing that the present writer and not a few others have been challenging this new doctrine, and largely upon the score of its entire novelty, for ten years past.[1]

Others, attempting to confuse the issue and to take the eyes of the premillennialist off the historicity of his faith, enumerate as many distinctions as possible between so-called historic premillennialism and modern premillennialism, which they sometimes call pretribulationism or dispensationalism. Allis, a lead-

[1] *The Gospel of the Kingdom,* p. 104.

ing amillennialist, is guilty of this, listing in his book nine
points in modern dispensationalism and asserting that:

> Of the nine points enumerated above, only the first two are
> entitled to be regarded as characteristic of Premillennialism
> historically understood. The remaining seven are distinctive of
> Dispensationalism.[2]

By doing this he is implying that because dispensationalism
differs greatly from premillennialism, in his estimation, it is
something recently introduced by Darby, Scofield, and others.

This double attack on premillennialism can be met without
difficulty. The contention that there is not a scrap of evidence
to support the historicity of the premillennial faith will be
adequately answered by the evidence to be presented in this
chapter. The other line of attack can be met by pointing out
that discovery and refinement of doctrine does not mean at
all that such doctrine is extra-Biblical. Conservative amillennialists would not deny that the great doctrines of the Reformation reclaimed by Luther and Calvin were "discovered" in
the sense that they were new and extra-Biblical. They would
admit, for instance, that the doctrine of satisfaction as set
forth by Anselm in the eleventh century was not so fully developed as it is today as seen in the writings of conservative
theologians. And yet they would not go on to conclude that
such recent refinements and developments in the doctrine of
the atonement are not to be received and believed simply because they are of recent origin. *Neither is there any reason to
reject recent findings in the field of eschatology.*

Turning again to the first line of attack, let us consider the

[2] *Op. cit.,* p. 9.

evidence for the historicity of premillennialism by tracing eschatological beliefs throughout the various periods of church history.

I. THE ANCIENT PERIOD

In the consideration of this period the teachings of the apostles themselves will not be included since these will be discussed later. Of the period of the apostolic fathers, Adolph Harnack, who is no special friend of premillennialism, says:

> Faith in the nearness of Christ's Second Advent and the establishing of His reign of glory on the earth was undoubtedly a strong point in the primitive Christian Church.[3]

Likewise, Philip Schaff, the great church historian, states:

> The most striking point in the eschatology of the ante-Nicene age is the prominent chiliasm, or millennarianism, that is the belief of a visible reign of Christ in glory on earth with the risen saints for a thousand years, before the general resurrection and judgment. It was indeed not the doctrine of the church embodied in any creed or form of devotion, but a widely current opinion of distinguished teachers.[4]

In addition to these general statements from noted historians, there is also an abundance of evidence from the writings of the period.

The Didache. The Didache, which is dated about 100 A.D., says concerning the Resurrection:

[3] "Millennium," *Encyclopaedia Britannica*, XV, 495.
[4] *History of the Christian Church*, II, 614.

And then shall appear the signs of the truth; first, the sign of an outspreading in heaven; then the sign of the sound of the trumpet; and the third, the resurrection of the dead; yet not of all.[5]

Although this quotation obviously does not prove premillennialism, it does show that the early Church did not teach a general resurrection as amillennialism does today.

Clement of Rome. The first letter by this man was written in 96 or 97 A.D. and was addressed to the Church at Corinth. In the letter is found this statement:

Of a truth, soon and suddenly shall His will be accomplished, as the Scriptures also bear witness, saying, "Speedily will He come, and will not tarry:" and "The Lord shall suddenly come to His temple, even the Holy One, for whom ye look." [6]

The Shepherd of Hermas. This document, written sometime between 140 and 150 A.D. says:

You have escaped from great tribulation on account of your faith, and because you did not doubt the presence of such a beast. Go, therefore, and tell the elect of the Lord His mighty deeds, and say to them that this beast is a type of the great tribulation that is coming.[7]

Since some have tried to deny that this man was chiliastic in belief, it should be mentioned that Berkhof, an amillennialist, admits that he was.[8]

Barnabas. Barnabas believed that the history of this world would be consummated after six thousand years. These six

[5] XVI: 6-7.
[6] *To the Corinthians*, XXIII.
[7] *Visions*, I, IV, 2.
[8] *Reformed Dogmatics*, p. 270.

days, as he called them, were to be concluded by the return of Christ to the earth at which time He would set up His kingdom on the earth for the seventh day of a thousand years of sabbath rest. During this time the temple was to be rebuilt by the servants of God's enemies and afterward the eighth day would begin the new world.[9] Recent amillennialists have claimed that this man was not a chiliast, but, although it is true that his system of teaching is not fully developed since his work is not large, his doctrine certainly leaves no room for amillennial eschatology.

Ignatius of Antioch. The date of the death of Ignatius, bishop of Antioch, falls somewhere between 50 and 115 A.D. He actually says very little along eschatological lines, but his references are understood by many writers to be in correspondence with chiliasm, for he refers to the "last times" and emphasizes the attitude of expectancy.[10]

Papias. Papias, bishop of Hierapolis (80-163), described the millennial fertility in superlative language as follows:

> The days will come in which vines shall grow, having each ten thousand branches, and in each branch ten thousand twigs, and in each true twig ten thousand shoots, and in every one of the shoots ten thousand clusters, and on every one of the clusters ten thousand grapes, and every grape when pressed will give five-and-twenty metretes of wine.[11]

In another place he declares that there will be a millennium after the Resurrection of the dead "when the personal reign of Christ will be established on the earth." [12]

[9] Chapter XV.
[10] Peters, *The Theocratic Kingdom,* I, 495.
[11] Fragment IV.
[12] Fragment VI.

Justin Martyr. This man of God (born about 100 A.D.) is an avowed premillennialist. He placed great importance on this hope and regarded the expectation of the earthly perfection of Christ's kingdom as the keystone of pure doctrine. He spoke of the Coming of Christ as preceded by the manifestation of the man of sin who would speak blasphemies against the most high God and who would rule three and a half years. In his *Dialogus cum Tryphone* he writes:

> But I and whoever are on all points right-minded Christians know that there will be resurrection of the dead and a thousand years in Jerusalem, which will then be built, adorned, and enlarged as the prophets Ezekiel and Isaiah and the others declare. . . .

> And, further, a certain man with us, named John, one of the Apostles of Christ, predicted by a revelation that was made to him that those who believed in our Christ would spend a thousand years in Jerusalem, and thereafter the general, or to speak briefly, the eternal resurrection and judgment of all men would likewise take place.[13]

Irenaeus. This man, bishop of Lyons, who died in 200 A.D., came in contact with apostolic teaching through his friend Polycarp. Thus the basis for his chiliastic beliefs is the teaching of the Apostle John and his disciples. Intricate detail characterizes his eschatological system. He says:

> But when this Antichrist shall have devastated all things in this world, he will reign for three years and six months, and sit in the temple at Jerusalem; and then the Lord will come from heaven in the clouds, in the glory of the Father, sending this man and those who followed him into the lake of fire; but bringing in for the righteous the times of the kingdom, that is,

[13] Chapters LXXX-LXXXI.

the rest, the hallowed seventh day; and restoring to Abraham the promised inheritance, in which kingdom the Lord declared, that "many coming from the east and from the west should sit down with Abraham, Isaac, and Jacob." . . .

The predicted blessing, therefore, belongs unquestionably to the times of the kingdom, when the righteous shall bear rule upon their rising from the dead.[14]

Tertullian. Tertullian (150-225) was undoubtedly a premillenarian also, for he says:

But we do confess that a kingdom is promised to us upon the earth, although before heaven, only in another state of existence; inasmuch as it will be after the resurrection for a thousand years in the divinely-built city of Jerusalem.[15]

The extent of the premillennial belief in the first two centuries of the history of the Church is well summarized by the historian Fisher who says:

The belief in a millennial kingdom on earth, to follow the second advent of Christ, was widely diffused.[16]

In the face of such overwhelming evidence, who can deny that premillennialism was the faith of the early church?

In the next three centuries of the ancient period, chiliastic beliefs declined. There are several reasons for this. First of all, when Constantine (272-337) became emperor of the entire Roman empire, he ended the early persecutions of the Church and united church and state. Immediately the Church found

---

[14] *Against Heresies,* V, XXX-XXXIII.
[15] *Against Marcion,* III, XXV.
[16] *History of the Christian Church,* p. 84

herself confronted by new conditions. No longer poor but now overburdened with wealth and worldly honors, she saw that to maintain the doctrine of pilgrimage and separation and to hope for a coming King and an earthly kingdom would be extremely displeasing to Constantine. Thus patronage of the Church by the world and the resulting prosperity brought the great loss to the Church of the hope of the soon Coming of her Lord.

Hitherto the Scriptures had supported the Church in her separation from the world, but since that course had been changed, the interpretation of the Scriptures also had to be changed in order to justify her position. Consequently, the rise of the Alexandrian school was a major factor in the rejection of chiliastic beliefs. Origen, the theologian of this school, openly attacked chiliasm and introduced the allegorical method of interpretation by which he interpreted spiritually and not literally the passages of Scripture which announced the millennium. Dionysius of Alexandria, a disciple of Origen, continued his teaching and prepared the ground for the rejection of the book of Revelation in 360 by the Council of Laodicea.

The third important factor in the rise of anti-chiliastic beliefs in this period was Augustine (354-430), bishop of Hippo. In brief, his position was as follows: the first resurrection is the rising of dead souls into spiritual life beginning with the ministry of Christ, from which time the millennium dates; the devil is bound and expelled from the hearts of Christ's disciples; the reign of the saints is their personal victory over sin and the devil; the beast is this wicked world and his image is hypocrisy; the millennium will end in 650 A.D., terminating the six-thousandth-year period and introducing the rise of Antichrist.

The truth, however, was not extinct, for several men in this period are outstanding in their defense of premillennialism.

Cyprian. This man (195-258) was a chiliast of strong persuasion who wrote graphically of the imminence of the kingdom of God and the certainty of the reign of Christ. For instance, he said:

> Why with frequently repeated prayers do we entreat and beg that the day of His kingdom may hasten, if our greater desires and stronger wishes are to obey the devil here, rather than to reign with Christ? [17]

Commodianus. This bishop of North Africa, who wrote about 250 A.D., made statements like these:

> They shall come also who overcame cruel martyrdom under Antichrist, and they themselves live for the whole time. But from the thousand years God will destroy all those evils.[18]

Nepos. This eminent and spiritual Egyptian bishop (230-250) wrote in defense of chiliasm after Origen's attack on it. His chief work is *A Confutation of the Allegorists,* which is specifically directed against those who were explaining the millennium figuratively. Concerning him, another has said:

> Nepos's views have been denominated sensual, but like many others of the Millennary Fathers, he has probably been misrepresented and misunderstood. That he was a Pre-millennialist is most certain, even Whitby allowing that Nepos taught "after this (first) resurrection the Kingdom of Christ was to be upon earth a thousand years, and the saints were to reign with him." [19]

[17] *On Morality,* XVIII.
[18] *Instructions,* XLIV.
[19] Taylor, *The Voice of the Church on the Reign of Christ,* p. 75.

Coracion. This man (c. 230-280) is usually considered to be a chiliast because he is linked with Nepos by various writers. It was he who took the place of Nepos after his death.

Methodius. The position of this man is inferred to be that of a chiliast because of his opposition to Origen.

Lactantius. The learned Latin father (240-330) was definitely a chiliast, for he wrote:

> About the same time also the prince of the devils, who is the contriver of all evils, shall be bound with chains, and shall be imprisoned during the thousand years of the heavenly rule in which righteousness shall reign in the world, so that he may contrive no evil against the people of God.[20]

Thus, concerning the ancient period we conclude that (1) in the first and purest centuries the Church was premillennial in her belief, and (2) with the coming of the union of Church and state the hope began to fade though it was not completely lost.

II. THE MEDIEVAL PERIOD

The Middle Ages was a period of gross darkness for all doctrines, and premillennialism was no exception. It has been shown that premillennialism was the historic faith of the early church, and this is most important, for it makes secondary the fact that the true doctrine was eclipsed during the Middle Ages. The basis of the premillennial faith is already well established in history, but for the sake of completeness its continued historical development will be traced.

[20] *Divine Institutes,* VII, XXIV.

The doctrine of the kingdom, as held by the early Church, was almost exterminated under the teaching and power of the papacy. However, as the year 1000 drew near, hopes for a speedy end of the world revived. Though this was proclaimed by various preachers, the position of organized Christianity was so strong in the world that the desire for the inauguration of a new order lost its vitality. Traditional millennial beliefs were perpetuated, but in general throughout the Middle Ages Christians were content with the triumph of the Church in the present order and with the hope for the individual soul after death.

However, the light of the truth was not totally extinguished, though there is no doubt but that it was brought into such disfavor by the ruling church of Rome that it was scarcely known in this period. Still there are intimations that the premillennial belief was held by some individuals and groups in some of its features, but even the truth in this age was mixed with error, for the darkness of Rome was deep and widespread.

The Waldensians. These holy people were banished and persecuted by the Roman church. Though they did not possess a well-developed system of eschatology, they were firm believers in the literal interpretation of Scripture and did look for the Coming of the Lord. *The Noble Lesson,* one of their writings, certainly shows their expectation of the coming kingdom.[21] The lack of a detailed system may be due in part to their point of emphasis which was directed against the Roman teaching that the Roman church was the kingdom and executor of judgment. But whatever they lacked in a system was com-

---

[21] Taylor, *op. cit.,* p. 131.

pensated by their looking for and loving of the appearance of the Lord.

The Paulicians. Though not chiliastic in the sense that the early church was, these people likewise looked for the Lord's Coming and the introduction of the age to come. The Cathari, successors of the Paulicians, shared similar views.

Of the nature of the evidence in this period we may conclude that it is not strong since it presents little by way of an eschatological system, but that it chiefly centers rather in the expectation of the return of Christ.

III. THE REFORMATION PERIOD

During the Reformation (1500-1650) there was a partial return to premillennial truth. In general, it may be said that the Reformers were not premillennialists, but their eschatology was overwhelmingly that of the Roman church from which they separated. Wycliffe, Calvin, Luther, Zwingli, and Melanchthon belong to this group. However, these men did look for the return of Christ though they believed that the Church was in some sense the kingdom of God. It should be remembered that they themselves acknowledged their liability to error and admitted that many things in the Bible were still obscure to them. Unquestionably their labors were not chiefly in the field of eschatology.

There were certain groups, however, that were definitely premillennial. In mentioning them it would be well to keep in mind this warning which Peters expresses:

It is unfortunate and misleading, that . . . efforts are made to link ancient and modern Chiliasm with the vagaries of Anabaptists and the Fifth Monarchy men, and *to infer hastily* that when these are confessionally or otherwise condemned by the Reformers and others, that *this also* is condemnatory of Chiliasm in all its phases. Such a line of procedure if applied to other doctrine, would leave but little for us to receive.[22]

Chiliasts in England. Several men in England may be considered chiliasts of this period although some were undoubtedly more profound and discerning in their beliefs than others. William Tyndale (1480-1536) is especially remembered for his insistence on the literal interpretation of Scripture. Nicholas Ridley and Hugh Latimer who were both burned at the stake in 1555 held chiliastic views. The latter said:

Peradventure it may come in my days, old as I am, or in my children's days. . . . The saints "shall be taken up to meet Christ in the air," and so shall come down with Him again. "He will put down Satan, that old Serpent, under our feet." [23]

By the end of the Reformation premillennialism in England had come into disrepute because its teaching had crystallized into a definite political propaganda known as the Fifth Monarchy Movement, which was bitterly antagonistic to Cromwell. Its advocates professed allegiance to King Jesus only, affirming that he was about to appear and establish a fifth world monarchy. They believed further that they should demonstrate their fitness by fighting for King Jesus, which conviction was expressed in two unsuccessful attempts at insurrection in 1657 and 1661.

Chiliasm in France. The Huguenots, a very spiritual people, were chiliasts, and this is one of the reasons the Roman church

[22] *Op. cit.,* I, 525.
[23] Silver, *The Lord's Return,* p. 123.

hated them so. The Camisards and the French prophets who flourished after the Reformation in France were also of chiliastic persuasion.[24]

Other chiliastic groups. Zurich, Switzerland, was the original home of the Anabaptists who were undoubtedly chiliasts. The Bohemian and Moravian Brethren, firmly allied with the Anabaptists, held the same faith relative to the premillennial return of Christ.

In summarizing this period, it may be said that although the Reformation did not bring a complete return to the premillennial hope, there was a partial return. That this return was often among sects that were later condemned does not imply that the doctrine itself is erroneous. Protestantism has never fully recovered from the eschatology of the Roman Catholic church as it was developed during the Middle Ages.

IV. THE MODERN PERIOD

The modern period has witnessed a mixture of beliefs. First it has seen the rise and fall of postmillennialism. Although its roots may be traced to Augustine, the father of modern postmillennialism is Daniel Whitby. The theory has already been outlined and does not have many adherents today. Amillennialism has flourished in the modern era with the weight of such men as B. B. Warfield, L. Berkhof, O. T. Allis, etc., behind it.

Premillennialism in Europe. It would be impossible to list all the exponents of premillennialism in the modern period. In his day alone, Peters could list by name at least 470 widely

---

[24] *Ibid.,* p. 125.

known ministers and writers in Europe who were premillennialists. Nevertheless, certain men were especially instrumental in bringing forth a return to the old historic faith in all its essentials.

Joseph Mede (1586-1638) who by his study was forced to yield to a literal interpretation of Scripture said:

> Yet this much I conceive the text seems to imply, that these *saints of the first resurrection should reign here on earth in the new Jerusalem* in a state of beatitude and glory, partaking of divine presence and vision of Christ their king.[25]

In 1740 a German, J. A. Bengel, issued a commentary on the Revelation which gave impetus to premillennialism in the scholarly world. John Wesley adopts Bengel's notes on the Revelation in his own commentary on the New Testament and therefore aligns himself with premillennialists. Also included among the prominent European chiliasts are these men who have written commentaries on all or portions of the Scriptures: Bengel, Olshausen, Gill, Stier, Alford, Lange, Meyer, Starke, Fausset, Bonar, Ryle, Seiss, Cumming, Delitzsch, Ebrard, Mede, Goodwin, Elliott, Cunningham, and Darby.

Premillennialism in America. In this country premillennialism was early incorporated into the belief of many of the first preachers. Outstanding among them is Increase Mather (1639-1723). This Puritan divine said in his book, *The Mystery of Israel's Salvation Explained and Applied:*

> That which presseth me so, as that I cannot gainsay the Chiliastical opinion, is that I take these four things for Principles, and no way doubt but that they are demonstrable. 1.

[25] Taylor, *op. cit.*, p. 171.

That the thousand apocalyptical years are not passed but future. 2. That the coming of Christ to raise the dead and to
judge the earth will be within much less than this thousand
years. 3. That the conversion of the Jews will not be till this
present state of the world is near unto its end. 4. That, after
the Jews' conversion there will be a glorious day for the elect
upon earth, and that this day shall be a very long continuance.[26]

His son, Cotton Mather (1663-1728) was also explicit in his
teaching:

It is well known, that in the earliest of the primitive times
the faithful did, in a literal sense, believe the "second coming"
of the Lord Jesus Christ, and the rising and the reigning of the
saints with Him, a thousand years *before,* the rest of the dead
live again. . . . The doctrine of the Millennium *is truth.*[27]

In addition, Mather also testifies that many of his contem-
poraries held premillennial views, and since his time scores
have embraced this truth. Peters lists at least 360 prominent
men in America who are premillennialists. In 1870 the book
Maranatha by James H. Brookes appeared and did much to
spread premillennialism. In 1878 W. E. Blackstone's *Jesus Is
Coming* was published, and it likewise influenced many believers. The *Scofield Reference Bible,* published first in 1909,
has probably been one of the greatest forces in popularizing
premillennial teachings. Today, premillennialists are a very
respectable minority in the Church and include many of the
ablest, most devoted, and scholarly men that the Church has
produced.

[26] Quoted by Smith, *Bibliotheca Sacra,* C, 76-77.
[27] Quoted by Peters, *op. cit.,* I, 542.

V. CONCLUSION

Most of the discussion in this chapter centered in the ancient period of church history, for it was deemed of utmost importance to show that premillennialism was the faith of the early church. Ample testimony was given to show that this was true in the first and purest centuries of the Church. The truth was practically lost in the Middle Ages, and even the Reformation brought only a partial return. In the modern period the return has not been complete, but the truth as held today is essentially the same as that which was held by the ancient church. The assertion by Mauro[28] that premillennialism has no basis in history plainly shows his ignorance of the facts. Certain refinements may be of recent origin, but premillennialism was certainly the faith of the Church centuries before the Brethren and Darby. The assertion that premillennialism is a new thing is not at all warranted in the light of the historical evidence. Premillennialism has a very solid basis in history.

[28] *Cf. ante.*

Chapter 3

Its Basis in
HERMENEUTICS

Hermeneutics is the science which teaches the principles of interpretation. Biblical hermeneutics in particular is the science which determines the principles of the interpretation of the Holy Scriptures. Hermeneutics is not exegesis, for exegesis is the practice of an art of which hermeneutics is the governing science. Hermeneutics, therefore, is the more basic science.

If it is to be shown that premillennialism is a Biblical doctrine, there must first be laid a foundation in a right understanding of hermeneutics, so that a proper exegesis may be built thereupon; hence, this discussion of hermeneutics as a basis of the premillennial faith is essential to the subsequent argument.

I. IMPORTANCE OF HERMENEUTICS

Harnack admits that in recent times a "mild type of 'academic' chiliasm has been developed from a belief in the verbal inspiration of the Bible." [1] While it is recognized that inspiration is not equivalent to hermeneutics, yet it is insisted that the former is a prerequisite to the latter. Although it could not be

[1] Harnack, *op. cit.*, XV, 497.

said that all amillennialists deny the verbal, plenary inspiration of the Scriptures, yet, as it will be shown later, it seems to be the first step in that direction. The system of spiritualizing Scripture is a tacit denial of the doctrine of the verbal, plenary inspiration of the Scriptures which this author holds. Nevertheless, it is significant that Harnack, no friend of premillennialism, links so closely verbal inspiration with premillennialism.

Assuming the verbal, plenary inspiration of Scripture, notice how crucial is the character of the issue concerning the science of hermeneutics in relation to premillennialism. The issue concerns the literal versus the figurative interpretation of Scripture. Hospers quotes Pieters, who is an amillennialist, in the foreword to his book on hermeneutics to show that principles of interpretation are determinative in the controversy. Pieters says:

> The question whether the Old Testament prophecies concerning the people of God must be interpreted in their ordinary sense, as other Scriptures are interpreted, or can properly be applied to the Christian Church, is called the question of the spiritualization of prophecy. This is one of the major problems in biblical interpretation, and confronts everyone who makes a serious study of the Word of God. It is one of the chief keys to the difference of opinion between Premillenarians and the mass of Christian scholars. The former reject such spiritualization, the latter employ it; and as long as there is no agreement on this point the debate is interminable and fruitless.[2]

Hamilton, another amillennialist, confesses:

> Now we must frankly admit that a literal interpretation of the Old Testament prophecies gives us just such a picture of an earthly reign of the Messiah as the premillennialist pictures.[3]

[2] *The Principle of Spiritualization in Hermeneutics,* p. 5.
[3] *Op. cit.,* p. 38.

It is little wonder then that Rutgers, too, another amillennialist, regards the premillennialist's interpretation of Scripture as the fundamental error of the system. Thus, it is clear that the question of interpretation is a basic and crucial one which demands careful consideration. It can either make or break the premillennial system.

II. GENERAL PRINCIPLES OF INTERPRETATION

There are certain definite and recognized principles of Biblical interpretation which will be stated first. Then it can be shown how closely the premillennial interpretation adheres to these general principles. This is the proper and logical order, though amillennialism reverses it, stating its system first and then formulating principles of interpretation which will work for that system. All doctrine must be built on sound principles of interpretation; otherwise, the doctrine must be changed. These are the general principles of hermeneutics.

Interpret grammatically. There is no more basic rule of interpretation than this. The interpreter must begin his work by studying the grammatical sense of the text, determining the exact meaning of the words according to linguistic usage and connection. A word is the vehicle of a thought; therefore, the meaning of any passage must be determined by a study of the words therein with the relationship sustained in the sentence. This is a natural corollary to the belief in the verbal, plenary inspiration of Scripture, for if one holds that the words of the text were inspired of God, then one must interpret those very words. A true exegesis is demanded.

Interpret according to the context. The Bible is not a book of words or verses put together without any relation to one another. Therefore, the context, which includes both the immediate context and the wider scope of the section or book, must be studied in order to see the relation that each verse sustains to that which precedes and to that which follows. Nothing is better than to have an author explain himself, and the study of the context is one of the most trustworthy resources at the command of the interpreter. Sometimes the immediate context does not give all the needed light on a certain passage, and so the wider context, even the scope of the book itself, must be considered. The purpose of the writing, the people addressed, and the general theme of the book are all important factors. The later discussion of the new covenant in Hebrews 8 will afford a good example of this rule.

Compare Scripture with Scripture. This principle of interpretation, which was not employed until the Reformation, places hermeneutics on a true and solid foundation. It not only uses parallel passages in Scripture but also regulates the interpretation of each passage in conformity with the whole tenor of revealed truth. It brings low those who claim to receive the Bible as the Word of God, and who reject specific revelations in it because they do not fit into the framework of their preconceived theology. It is a great inconsistency to admit a positive revelation and then to reject things positively revealed. The application of this principle of hermeneutics means the harmonization of all the Bible. An obscure or seemingly contradictory passage cannot invalidate a doctrine clearly supported by this principle of the analogy of faith. Amillennialists who ridicule obscure points in the premillennial system should not forget that they have yet to produce, even in outline form, a system concerning which there is unanimous agreement among their own group.

These, then, are the general principles of interpretation. What use does premillennialism make of these general principles? Does it practice what it preaches? That premillennialism interprets grammatically, that is, literally, is undisputed, for this is the major point of difference, readily admitted, between premillennialism and amillennialism. It does appeal to the context, as in the example cited; and there is no question but that premillennialism claims to have a complete system which follows the rule of comparing Scripture with Scripture.

It is evident from amillennial commentaries and theologies that they accept a literal interpretation of most of the Bible, but in the field of eschatology they resort to the principle of spiritualization. Thus the system is in the position of using two different and contradictory principles of interpretation. It is useless, then, for amillennialists to argue against and object to premillennialism when the basic rules of interpretation are not established. Nevertheless, since the two systems do agree on general principles, the crux of the matter must lie in the field of principles of the interpretation of prophecy.

III. PRINCIPLES OF INTERPRETATION OF PROPHECY

All acknowledge the necessity for a valid rule for the interpretation of prophecy. Hamilton says typically:

> There are many passages in prophecy which were meant to be taken literally. In fact a good working rule to follow is that the literal interpretation of prophecy is to be accepted unless

(a) the passages contain obviously figurative language, or (b) unless the New Testament gives authority for interpreting them in other than a literal sense, or (c) unless a literal interpretation would produce a contradiction.[4]

Spiritualizing, then, is the answer of the amillennialist to the problem of the interpretation of prophecy. It is the same as allegorizing, and this method of interpretation does not have a savory origin. Farrar, who is no premillennialist, points out:

Allegory by no means sprang from spontaneous piety, but was the child of Rationalism which owed its birth to the heathen theories of Plato. It deserved its name, for it made Scripture say something else than it really meant. . . .

Origen borrows from heathen Platonists and from Jewish philosophers a method which converts the whole of Scripture, alike the New and the Old Testament, into a series of clumsy, varying, and incredible enigmas. Allegory helped him to get rid of Chiliasm and superstitious literalism and the "antitheses" of the Gnostics, but it opened the door for deadlier evils.[5]

This raises a grave question at the very outset as to the integrity of this spiritualizing method of interpreting prophecy. Hamilton's reasons for spiritualizing Scripture are easily answered. The figures for which the figurative language stands have a literal fulfillment. Many of the New Testament passages adduced as examples of spiritual interpretation of the Old Testament are merely citations of proof texts by Scripture writers in support of specific points. Finally, there is no justification for departing from the literal sense of Scripture because

---

[4] *Op. cit.,* p. 53.
[5] *History of Interpretation,* pp. 193-194, 196.

that sense creates an apparent contradiction. Many of these apparent contradictions will be discussed in the pages to follow, but it suffices to point out here that if contradictions justify rejection of the system, then amillennialism as a system must be rejected, for it has serious contradictions which still await solution.

But, it may well be asked, how does the premillennialist meet the problem of the interpretation of prophecy? Are there any special principles for the interpretation of prophecy which he employs but which are in accord with the basic hermeneutical principle of literal interpretation? These questions are answered by the following list of special principles for the interpretation of prophecy, which principles are consistent with, not contradictory to, the general principles of hermeneutics already discussed. These are not principles deduced from premillennial exegesis, but rather these are special rules growing out of the general rules of hermeneutics and the particular problem of prophecy upon which premillennial exegesis is based. If, then, these special principles which concern interpretation of prophecy are consistent with the basic law of hermeneutics, that is, literal interpretation, and if they point the way to a comprehensive, consistent, and harmonious system of Biblical interpretation, then premillennialism rests on an exceedingly firm basis in relation to hermeneutics.

Consistency in principle. This is a summary statement of that which has just been said. Prophecy is not a special case in that it demands special hermeneutics if such a system contradicts the basic principle of literal interpretation. There may be special outworkings of that principle but the principle must be consistent.

Compare prophecy with prophecy. This very fundamental principle of prophetic interpretation is enjoined by the Scripture itself, for Peter says, "Knowing this first, that no prophecy of the scripture is of any private interpretation" (2 Pet. 1:20). Ἰδίας is generally used in the sense of "one's own" (John 1:11; 1 Cor. 12:11; Matt. 14:13), and it simply means that no prophecy is to be interpreted by itself, but in the light of all that God has spoken on the subject. Every prophecy is part of a wonderful scheme of revelation, and this entire scheme as well as the interrelationship between the parts must be kept in mind. No one prophet received the revelation of all the truth; rather, the Book unfolds little by little, without contradiction, until we have a complete and perfect picture. In this connection it must be remembered that difficulties are not contradictions. Neither does the existence of a problem militate against the plain statements of prophecy. In dealing with such problems, Feinberg offers two pertinent suggestions:

> First of all, when certain difficulties are affirmed of a doctrine which claims to be Biblical, one is only required to show that a solution of the alleged problem is possible. When certain passages are referred to which are said to contradict the premillennial doctrine, all that is necessary is to demonstrate that according to the rules of exegesis, a harmonization is possible. Secondly, sometimes even this cannot be fairly required. If any doctrine is shown on the basis of the laws of exegesis to be taught in the Bible, then to prove the doctrine false more is needed than the mere statement that the teaching brings to light even unanswerable problems. Otherwise, it could be demonstrated that the doctrines of salvation and redemption are false. The same method is used in rejecting and denying these doctrines that is employed in opposing premillennialism. In order to disprove premillennial interpretation of Scripture, its

opponents must show that its exegesis of the passages of Scripture involved is false and erroneous.[6]

Interpretation differs from application. Interpretation is one; application is manifold. The primary aim of the interpreter is, in every case, to discover the true and only interpretation. Literal interpretation allows wide latitude in making spiritual applications from all passages, but there are two extremes to be avoided in applying this principle. Some have made so much of application that the true interpretation has been lost. This is usually a pathway to amillennialism. Others, and premillennialists are often guilty of this, have been so intent on discovering the interpretation that they have lost all application along with the resultant blessing. Psalm 122:6 may well be used as an example of the proper distinction between interpretation and application. The verse reads: "Pray for the peace of Jerusalem: they shall prosper that love thee." The literal interpreter understands this verse in a twofold sense: (1) the primary reference is to the city Jerusalem and that for which it, as the capital, stands representative, that is, the nation Israel and the land, and (2) there is also a secondary application, but not interpretation, allowed, that is, an expression of the general truth that in all generations divine blessing has rested upon all who forwarded the work of those identified with the Lord. The application, however, does not in any way take the place of the interpretation.

Figurative language. Although much of prophecy is given in plain terms, much of it is in figurative language, and this constitutes a problem of interpretation. It may be said as a general statement that the use of figurative language does not

[6] *Premillennialism or Amillennialism?*, pp. 35-36.

compromise or nullify the literal sense of the thing to which it is applied. Figures of speech are a legitimate grammatical usage for conveying a literal meaning. More specifically, in interpreting figures of speech, it may be said, as Patrick Fairbairn does, that:

> . . . care should be taken to give a fair and natural, as opposed to a far-fetched or fanciful, turn to the figure employed. We do so, on the ground, that figurative language is essentially of a popular caste, and is founded on those broader and more obvious resemblances, which do not need to be searched for, but are easily recognised and generally used.[7]

Premillennialists' use of types often brings criticism in this connection. The use of types is perfectly legitimate as illustration of the truth though they should not be used to teach doctrine. All literalists recognize numerous types in prophecy, but they insist on solid, grammatical interpretation. It is one thing to say that Israel *typifies* the Church, as premillennialists rightly do; it is quite another thing to say that Israel *is* the Church, as amillennialists wrongly teach.

Figures of speech, then, give no cause for spiritualizing Scripture. Hospers says:

> It must be noted that opponents of Premillenarianism often confuse matters by an equivocation of the legitimate figures of speech with their own artificial conception of spiritualization.[8]

Citing Galatians 4:24-26 as a specific example, he further says:

> It is Paul's allegory. As already stated above, according to good rhetoric, an allegory is an extended metaphor. We must

[7] *Hermeneutical Manual,* p. 148.
[8] *Op. cit.,* p. 10.

therefore sharply discriminate between taking allegory as equivalent to spiritualization and as regular figurative speech. In the passage Paul uses geographical terms by means of which he illustrated. Lightfoot puts it well: "With St. Paul, on the other hand, Hagar's career is an allegory because it is history. The symbol and the thing symbolized are the same in kind. . . . With Philo the allegory is the whole substance of his teaching; with St. Paul it is but an accessory. He uses it rather as an illustration than an argument." [9]

In conclusion it may be stated that in connection with the use of figurative language, the interpreter should look not for the literal sense of the words employed in the figure, but for the literal sense intended by the use of the figure. Figurative language does not make void literal interpretation.

Law of fulfillment. In the interpretation of unfulfilled prophecy, fulfilled prophecy forms the pattern. The logical way to discover how God will fulfill prophecy in the future is to discover how He fulfilled it in the past. If the hundreds of prophecies concerning Christ's first coming were fulfilled literally, how can anyone reject the literal fulfillment of the numerous prophecies concerning His Second Coming and reign on the earth? Feinberg cites a pertinent example:

Take, for example, the words of Gabriel in the first chapter of Luke where he foretells of the birth of Christ. According to the angel's words Mary literally conceived in her womb; literally brought forth a son; His name was literally called Jesus; He was literally great; and He was literally called the Son of the Highest. Will it not be as literally fulfilled that God will yet give to Christ the throne of His father David, that He will reign over the house of Jacob forever, and that of His glorious kingdom there shall be no end? [10]

9 *Ibid.*, pp. 21-22.
10 *Op. cit.*, p. 39.

How inconsistent it is, then, to apply any kind of special hermeneutics to the prophecies of the Second Coming when there was no need of doing so with the prophecies of His first coming.

Law of double reference. Often a prophecy may have a double fulfillment, one being in the immediate circumstances and another in the distant future. Christ's being called great and the Son of the Highest, in the example cited above, has a double fulfillment. These things were literally true at His first coming, but they were not universally true as they will be at His Second Coming. The Psalms furnish many examples of this law, and amillennialists admit that there are many references which do not have an adequate explanation in the immediate experiences of David and which therefore point to a future fulfillment by David's greater Son. Nevertheless, double fulfillment is literal fulfillment and is therefore consistent with the basic rules of interpretation.

Law of time relationship. This law may assume several forms. Two or more events of a like character may be described in a common profile. The prophecy of Rachel's mourning for her children is an example of this. Scripture reveals that this applies to the Babylonian captivity in the first instance and to the slaughter of the innocent children under Herod in the second instance (Jer. 31:15; Matt. 2:18).

This law takes another form when future events are so mingled together on the horizon of prophecy as to appear like mountains in a range of mountains, the valleys being hidden. Simply because two events are placed side by side is no proof that the fulfillment will take place simultaneously or even in immediate succession. Isaiah 9:6-8; 61:1-2; Daniel 9:24-27

are a few examples of these tremendous gaps of time in the
Scriptures.

IV. RESULTS AND CONCLUSION

Results of allegorical interpretation. Those who employ the
allegorical method of interpretation arrive at a diversity of interpretation. It is noteworthy that premillennialists and amillennialists agree on the main lines of truth whenever the
principle of literal interpretation is retained. The doctrines of
theology proper, sin, salvation, etc., are generally agreed on,
but in the doctrine of future things where the amillennialist
feels obliged to employ his allegorical interpretation there is
diversity. Not only is there diversity between the systems of
interpretation, but there is also diversity within amillennial
ranks. Such disagreement necessarily tends to discredit the
authority of the Scriptures in the eyes of the unsaved and of
the untaught.

Allegorical interpretation fosters modernism. As has often
been pointed out, it is almost impossible to find a premillennial
liberal or modernist. Among the Brethren, who are supposed
to be the founders of modern literalism, liberalism is practically
unknown. On the other hand, the great body of modernistic
Protestantism is avowedly amillennial. Thus the allegorical
method of amillennialism is a step toward modernism.

Finally, it should be pointed out that allegorical interpretation cannot explain the Scriptures. Of course, many doctrines
are explained by amillennialists, but in these the literal principle is followed. But in the field of eschatology even the amillennialist admits that "the doctrine of future things is still an

unexplored field." [11] This certainly cannot be said of premillennialism.

Results of literal interpretation. When the principles of literal interpretation both in regard to general and special hermeneutics are followed, the result is the premillennial system of doctrine. In contrast to the results noted above, there is general agreement among premillennialists on the main lines of prophetic truth; premillennialism is diametrically opposed to modernism; and premillennialism does not leave large portions of the Scripture unexplained. All explanations may not agree in every detail, but at least all portions of Scripture are treated.

Conclusion. In this chapter we have dealt with the basic issue. If one interprets literally, he arrives at the premillennial system. If one employs the spiritualizing or allegorizing method of interpretation in the field of eschatology, he arrives at amillennialism. There is no disagreement over the fundamental rules of interpretation—even though they spell literal interpretation; the disagreement is in the interpretation of prophecy. The amillennialist's answer is special hermeneutics which are special in the sense that they contradict all regular hermeneutical principles. The premillennialist's answer includes some special considerations in interpreting prophecy, but these are special in the sense that they are particularly useful only in prophetic interpretation while at the same time being harmonious with the basic principles of hermeneutics. Thus, premillennialism is solidly based in hermeneutics, and upon this solid foundation the remainder of this book is built.

[11] W. Masselink, *Why Thousand Years?*, p. 11.

Chapter 4

Its Basis in the
ABRAHAMIC COVENANT

In the next three chapters we shall consider the relationship to premillennialism of the Abrahamic, Davidic, and new covenants. It is a large task because so much material must be considered, but it is basic to the argument. If it can be demonstrated that any one of these covenants is still in force with respect to its promises, this will practically annul the amillennial system, for each of them contains promises which require a separate national future for Israel, including possession of the promised land. On the other hand, it is equally true that if any one of these covenants allows its future fulfillment to be by the Church, premillennialism is tremendously weakened, for it insists that the Church does not fulfill Israel's promises in any sense at all. The study of the covenants is vital to premillennialism. The Mosaic covenant does not enter into the argument, for all agree that it was conditioned upon Israel's obedience.

I. THE IMPORTANCE OF THE COVENANT

All agree that the Abrahamic covenant is one of the outstanding covenants in the Word of God. Its crucial issues in relation to premillennialism are two: (1) Does the Abrahamic covenant promise Israel a permanent existence as a nation? If it does, then the Church is not fulfilling Israel's promises, but rather Israel as a nation has a future yet in prospect; and (2) does the Abrahamic covenant promise Israel permanent possession of the promised land? If it does, then Israel must yet come into possession of that land, for she has never fully possessed it in her history. The answers to these two questions center around two other considerations: (1) Is the covenant conditional? This is a crucial issue, for if it can be proved conditional, then Israel has no assurance of a future national identity or possession of the land; and (2) if it is not conditional, how will those parts yet unfulfilled be fulfilled? Will they be fulfilled spiritually by the Church or literally by Israel? These are the important questions and issues relative to the Abrahamic covenant.

II. THE PROMISES OF THE COVENANT

The major passage setting forth the covenant is Genesis 12:1-3:

> Now the Lord had said unto Abram, Get thee out of thy country, and from thy kindred, and from thy father's house, unto a land that I will shew thee: And I will make of thee a great nation, and I will bless thee, and make thy name great; and thou shalt be a blessing: And I will bless them that bless thee, and curse him that curseth thee: and in thee shall all families of the earth be blessed.

The personal promises to Abraham include the special blessing of God, a great name, himself as a channel of divine blessing to others, a divine treatment of others on the basis of their attitude toward him, and an heir by Sarah (Gen. 15:4).

The national promises of which Abraham was given assurance were that his seed would be a great nation (*cf.* Gen. 17:6), the land of Canaan would be given for an everlasting inheritance (*cf.* Gen. 17:8), and the covenant would be established with his seed (Gen. 17:7).

There were also two universal promises given to Abraham: (1) the promise of divine treatment of others on the basis of their attitude toward Abraham, which is a universal as well as a personal promise, and (2) the principal universal promise that "in thee shall all the families of the earth be blessed."

III. THE HISTORIC FULFILLMENT OF THE COVENANT

It should be strikingly evident throughout this section that God's method in fulfilling parts of the Abrahamic covenant has been *literal*.

(1) In fulfillment of the personal promises, Abraham was specially blessed of God. Lincoln has pointed out:

a. Abraham was blessed personally in temporal things: (1) He had land (Gen. 13:14, 15, 17); (2) He had servants (Gen. 15:7, etc.); (3) He had much cattle, silver, and gold (Gen. 13:2; 24:34, 35).

b. Abraham was blessed personally in spiritual matters: (1) He had a happy life of separation unto God, (Gen. 13:8; 14:22, 23); (2) He enjoyed a precious life of communion with God, (Gen. 13:18); (3) He had a consistent life of prayer, (Gen. 28:23-33); (4) He was sustained of God constantly,

(Gen. 21:22); (5) He possessed the peace and confidence that comes from an obedient life, (Gen. 22:5, 8, 10, 12, 16-18).[1]

(2) He had a great name. Bush has said:

Not so much in the records of worldly fame, as in the history of the church. Yet it is a remarkable fact, that perhaps no mere man has ever been so widely and so permanently honoured. "The Jews, and many tribes of the Saracens and Arabians, justly own and revere him as their progenitor: many nations in the East exceedingly respect his memory to this day, and glory in their real or pretended relation to him. Throughout the visible church he has always been highly venerated; and even now Jews, Mohammedans, and many Gentiles vie with each other and with Christians, who shall most honour this ancient patriarch! Nothing could be more improbable at the time than this event; yet the prediction has been fulfilling, most exactly and minutely, during the course of almost four thousand years!" [2]

(3) He was a channel of divine blessing to others, for he not only blessed his household, his posterity, but the world at large through the Bible, the Saviour, and the gospel.

(4) History has borne out the fact that nations which have persecuted Israel, even when that very persecution was in fulfillment of God's discipline, have been punished for dealing with Abraham's seed. This has been true in both blessing and cursing in the case of the slaughter of the kings (Gen. 14:12-16); in the case of Melchizedek (Gen. 14:18-20); in the case of Abimelech (Gen. 20:2-18; 21:22-34); in the case of Heth (Gen. 23:1-20); and in other experiences in Israel's history (Deut. 30:7; Isa. 14:1-2; Joel 3:1-8; Matt. 25:40-45).

[1] "The Covenants," pp. 182-183.
[2] *Notes on Genesis,* pp. 195-196.

(5) Abraham did have an heir by Sarah (Gen. 21:2).

The national promises are the ones concerning which premillennialism has its controversy with other systems of interpretation and will be reserved for discussion under the unconditional character of the covenant, for these promises have not had their complete fulfillment.

The universal promise of blessing to all the families of the earth has been fulfilled. As Bush says:

> It is not wealth, fame, power, sensual pleasure, or mental endowments, but the gift of his own Son as a Saviour, the bestowment of the Holy Spirit, the pardon of sin, peace of conscience, and the high and purifying hopes connected with eternal life. This is the inheritance that makes us truly rich, and utterly vain, foolish, and fatal is it to seek for real *blessedness* from any other source.[3]

Denial that these aforementioned promises have been fulfilled is puerile. But the question of the fulfillment of the national promises still remains to be answered.

IV. THE UNCONDITIONAL CHARACTER
OF THE COVENANT

The unconditional character of the Abrahamic covenant is the crucial issue in making the Abrahamic covenant a basis for premillennialism. If the covenant is unconditional, then the national aspect of it must yet be fulfilled, and premillennialism is the only system of interpretation which makes a place for a national future for Israel in which she possesses her land.

Amillennialists are divided in their view of the covenant.

[3] *Ibid.*, p. 197.

Some accept its unconditional character but endeavor by spiritualizing to be rid of the objectionable portion of it. This is the view of Berkhof. Others, and these are greater in number, view the covenant as conditional and consequently in no need of fulfillment. This is the view of Allis and others. These arguments will be answered as we list the positive reasons advanced by premillennialists for the unconditional character of the covenant.

(1) The Abrahamic covenant is called eternal in the Word of God.

> And I will establish my covenant between me and thee in their generations for an everlasting covenant, to be a God unto thee, and to thy seed after thee. (Gen. 17:7)

> . . . and my covenant shall be in your flesh for an everlasting covenant. (Gen. 17:13b)

> And God said, Sarah thy wife shall bear thee a son indeed; and thou shalt call his name Isaac: and I will establish my covenant with him for an everlasting covenant, and with his seed after him. (Gen. 17:19)

> Even of the covenant which he made with Abraham, and of his oath unto Isaac; And hath confirmed the same to Jacob for a law, and to Israel for an everlasting covenant. (I Chron. 16:16-17)

> Which covenant he made with Abraham, and his oath unto Isaac; And confirmed the same unto Jacob for a law, and to Israel for an everlasting covenant. (Psa. 105:9-10)

The Scriptures clearly teach that this is an eternal covenant based on the gracious promises of God. There may be delays, postponements, and chastisements, but an eternal covenant cannot, if God cannot deny Himself, be abrogated.

(2) The original promises given to Abraham were given without any conditions whatsoever. The words recorded in Genesis 12 are clear in their testimony. Allis, the amillennialist, admits that:

It is true that, in the express terms of the covenant with Abraham, obedience is not stated as a condition.[4]

He then proceeds to contradict himself by attempting to show that obedience is a condition, by which action he is certainly not showing himself to be the Calvinist that he is when he speaks of security thus. In any case, the Scripture does not condition the original promises given to Abraham. Later confirmation in Scripture of the unconditional character will follow. However, it seems clear that the covenant as established was a unit. Galatians 3:15, "Though it be but a man's covenant, yet when it hath been confirmed, no one maketh it void nor addeth thereto," makes certain that the covenant may not be tampered with either by being added to or subtracted from. If, as Allis admits, the covenant is unconditional in its inception, then he should also admit that it remains unconditional throughout history. Who dares add conditions to the God-given content of the covenant?

(3) The covenant was confirmed by reiteration and enlargement. In Genesis 13:14-17, Abraham is promised title forever to all the land which he saw, and the promise concerning his seed is amplified in that he is promised seed comparable in number to the dust of the earth. In Genesis 15:1-7, the line of the seed is designated as coming through Abraham, not Eliezer,

[4] *Op. cit.,* p. 33.

his servant, and the promise of the land is reiterated. In Genesis 17:1-8, the covenant is solemnly confirmed, kings are promised to his seed, all the land of Canaan is given to the seed of Abraham for an everlasting possession, a personal and special relationship is set up between God and the seed of Abraham in which God promises to be their God, and Abram is given the name Abraham as a symbol of the promise that he will be the father of many nations, that is, nations other than the one which will inherit the land. This reiteration was doubtless for emphasis. It does not indicate any temporal character of the covenant, but supports the premillennialists' claims that the covenant is unconditional.

(4) The covenant was solemnized in a recognized way.

And he said unto him, Take me an heifer of three years old, and a ram of three years old, and a turtledove, and a young pigeon. And he took unto him all these, and divided them in the midst, and laid each piece one against another: but the birds divided he not. . . . And when the sun was going down, a deep sleep fell upon Abram; and, lo, an horror of great darkness fell upon him. . . . And it came to pass, that, when the sun went down, and it was dark, behold a smoking furnace, and a burning lamp that passed between those pieces. (Gen. 15:9, 10, 12, 17)

Commenting on this passage, Keil and Delitzsch say:

The proceeding corresponded rather to the custom, prevalent in many ancient nations, of slaughtering animals when concluding a covenant, and after dividing them into pieces, of laying the pieces opposite to one another, that the persons making the covenant might pass between them. Thus . . . God condescended to follow the custom of the Chaldeans, that He might in the most solemn manner confirm His oath to Abram

the Chaldean. The wide extension of this custom is evident
from the expression used to denote the conclusion of a covenant, כָּרַת בְּרִית to hew, or cut a covenant . . . whilst it is
evident from Jer. xxxiv. 18, that this was still customary among
the Israelites of later times.[5]

The unconditional character of the covenant is further emphasized by the fact that only Jehovah passed between the
parts of the sacrifice. Concerning this, these same scholars say:

> From the nature of this covenant, it followed, however, that
> God alone went through the pieces in a symbolical representa-
> tion of Himself, and not Abram also. For although a covenant
> always establishes a reciprocal relation between two individuals,
> yet in that covenant which God concluded with a man, the man
> did not stand on an equality with God, but God established the
> relation of fellowship by His promise and His gracious con-
> descension to the man.[6]

(5) The covenant was given a visible sign in the rite of circumcision (Gen. 17:9-14). The amillennialist uses this as
an argument to attempt to show that the covenant was conditional, for, according to him, since circumcision was a required
act of obedience the covenant must be conditional. The truth
is that circumcision was the personal act which related the man
to the covenant and had nothing to do with the unconditional
nature of the everlasting covenant. One uncircumcised person
certainly could not annul the covenant any more than one un-
believer can by his unbelief make void the grace of God for
everyone else.

(6) The Abrahamic covenant was confirmed by the birth
of Isaac and then confirmed to him.

[5] *The Pentateuch*, I, 214.
[6] *Ibid.*, I, 216.

> And God said, Sarah thy wife shall bear thee a son indeed; and thou shalt call his name Isaac: and I will establish my covenant with him for an everlasting covenant, and with his seed after him. (Gen. 17:19)

> For Sarah conceived, and bare Abraham a son in his old age, at the set time of which God had spoken to him. (Gen. 21:2)

> And the Lord appeared unto him [Isaac], and said, Go not down into Egypt; dwell in the land which I shall tell thee of: Sojourn in this land, and I will be with thee, and will bless thee; for unto thee, and unto thy seed, I will give all these countries, and I will perform the oath which I sware unto Abraham thy father; And I will make thy seed to multiply as the stars of heaven, and will give unto thy seed all these countries; and in thy seed shall all the nations of the earth be blessed. (Gen. 26:2-4)

No conditions are attached to this reiteration to Isaac of the covenant, for it is based on the unconditional oath of God to Abraham. Now Abraham had sinned during the years since the covenant was first made to him and the time when it was confirmed to Isaac, and if God had viewed the covenant as conditioned upon obedience, then there was ample reason for abrogating the entire covenant. Instead, however, He confirms His promise to Isaac, and thereby manifests the unconditional character of the Abrahamic covenant.

(7) The covenant was likewise confirmed to Jacob.

> And, behold, the Lord stood above it, and said, I am the Lord God of Abraham thy father, and the God of Isaac: the land whereon thou liest, to thee will I give it, and to thy seed; And thy seed shall be as the dust of the earth, and thou shalt spread abroad to the west, and to the east, and to the north, and to the south: and in thee and in thy seed shall all the families of the earth be blessed. And, behold, I am with thee, and will

keep thee in all places whither thou goest, and will bring thee again into this land; for I will not leave thee, until I have done that which I have spoken to thee of. (Gen. 28:13-15)

Again it should be noticed that the covenant was reaffirmed without any conditions attached showing again its unconditional character. (Since the promise was given to Jacob and his heirs, this answers the amillennialists' question, why is Esau excluded from the land if the covenant is unconditional?)

(8) The covenant was confirmed in spite of disobedience. This is the crucial test in regard to the unconditional character of the covenant, for amillennialists hold that disobedience is the ground on which it may be said that the covenant is no longer in force. But God said to Israel amid terrible apostasy:

Thus saith the Lord, which giveth the sun for a light by day, and the ordinances of the moon and of the stars for a light by night, which divideth the sea when the waves thereof roar; The Lord of hosts is his name: If these ordinances depart from before me, saith the Lord, then the seed of Israel also shall cease from being a nation before me for ever. Thus saith the Lord; if heaven above can be measured, and the foundations of the earth searched out beneath, I will also cast off all the seed of Israel for all that they have done, saith the Lord. (Jer. 31:35-37)

In spite of the apostasy, God graciously declares that His covenant has not been set aside. The Lord of hosts has put Himself on record, if language means anything at all, and has determined to fulfill His covenant in spite of disobedience.

(9) The Abrahamic covenant is unconditional because it is later used as the basis for giving the Palestinian covenant. The part of the Abrahamic covenant which relates to the land is

enlarged upon in the Palestinian covenant (Deut. 28:1-30:20) where the right to the enjoyment of the land is given. If the Abrahamic covenant which gives the title to the land were nullified, then the collateral doctrines in the Palestinian covenant would likewise be of no force, all of which would place God in the position of promising something to His people which He had already taken away from them because of disobedience. Of what meaning would be these promises, so similarly related to those of the Abrahamic covenant, if God had already abrogated that covenant? The Palestinian covenant, then, is a proof of the unconditional character of the Abrahamic covenant.

(10) Fulfillment of the Abrahamic covenant is not equivalent to enjoyment of that covenant. Simply because the children of Israel did not enjoy the promises and provisions of the covenant does not mean that these promises will not be fulfilled. Because of sin and disobedience they were often estranged from the promises, but never divorced from them. Similarly, the promises of God in this age of grace are not abrogated simply because the individual Christian believer fails to appropriate and enjoy them. How much more certain is fulfillment in the case of the promises of the Abrahamic covenant which promises are not based upon human appropriation but upon the immutable word and promise of the unchanging God.

(11) Unstated conditions cannot be construed to mean that conditions are nevertheless involved. This is a negative argument and is considered here only because amillennialists make so much of it. The command to Jonah is often given as an illustration of a condition implied, though not stated, because through his preaching the destruction of Nineveh was delayed.

However, the cases are not at all similar. In the case of Jonah it was a message; in the case of Abraham it was an everlasting covenant. The judgment of Eli's house (1 Sam. 2:30) is also used as an illustration of this alleged truth. Since God declared that Aaron's house would be the perpetual priesthood, and since Eli was cut off and Samuel installed in the priestly office, it is argued that obedience is implied as a condition. Remember, however, that the Aaronic priesthood was set up under the Mosaic covenant, which was very definitely conditional, while the Abrahamic covenant is unconditional. Unstated conditions are not implied in the Abrahamic covenant which supports the fact of its unconditional character.

(12) Since the covenant has never been fulfilled in history, if language means anything at all, it must have a future fulfillment. Amillennialists contend that the land was fully possessed by Israel during the time of Solomon. Their proof text is 1 Kings 4:21 which says:

> And Solomon reigned over all kingdoms from the river unto the land of the Philistines, and unto the border of Egypt: they brought presents, and served Solomon all the days of his life.

In the very fact of using this text the amillennialist is admitting that the covenant was *literally* fulfilled! Why, then, does he look for a spiritual fulfillment by the Church? However, we can point out four things which were not fulfilled by Solomon. There was no permanent possession of the land as promised to Abraham. All the land was not possessed. "From the river of Egypt" (Gen. 15:18) and "from the border of Egypt" (1 Kings 4:21) are not equivalent terms geographically. Solomon did not occupy all this land; he merely collected tribute. Temporary overlordship is not everlasting possession. Finally, hundreds of years after Solomon's time the Scriptures still abound in promises concerning future possession of the land. This must prove that God and His prophets realized, whether the amillennialist does or not, that Solomon had not fulfilled the Abrahamic covenant.

In closing this section concerning the unconditional character of the Abrahamic covenant verified by these twelve reasons, these words of Walvoord are appropriate:

> If God had intended to convey the impression that the covenant was eternal and unalterable, He could not have used more express and specific language. It is stated that His promises stand *in spite of* Israel's sins, and that they are unaltered by them. His promise is declared to be immutable: "Wherein God, being minded to show more abundantly unto the heirs of the promise the immutability of his counsel, interposed with an oath: that by two immutable things, in which it is impossible for God to lie, we may have strong encouragement, who have fled for refuge to lay hold of the hope set before us" (Heb. 6:17, 18; *cf.* 6:13-16).[7]

V. THE FUTURE FULFILLMENT OF THE COVENANT

Up to this point we have established two important facts. First, it has been shown that not all the promises given to Abraham have been fulfilled, specifically, the national promises. Secondly, it has been conclusively proved that the Abrahamic covenant is unconditional. The question now is, how are these two facts to be reconciled except the covenant have a future

[7] *Bibliotheca Sacra*, CII, 32.

fulfillment of some sort? All admit that some of the promises of the Abrahamic covenant have been fulfilled, but those who believe that the covenant is conditional hold that the spiritual aspects of it are fulfilled by the Church. It is true that:

> It may be conceded that some of the promises given to Abraham are intended to extend to the church. The individuals in the church enter into the promises of blessing given to those in Christ and to this extent are the spiritual children of Abraham. This is expressly stated in Scripture: "Know therefore that they which are of faith, the same are the sons of Abraham" (Gal. 3:7). The basis for this statement in Galatians, however, is not on any promise given to Israel—and this is very significant. The passage continues: "And the scripture, foreseeing that God would justify the Gentiles by faith, preached the gospel beforehand unto Abraham, saying, In thee shall all the nations be blessed. So then they that are of faith are blessed with the faithful Abraham" (Gal. 3:7-9). In other words, the portion of the covenant specifically given to Israel is not transferred to the church. Only the portion of the covenant dealing with the universal blessing such as extended beyond Israel is applicable to the church.[8]

The concession made above concerns only the universal promises given to Abraham and not the national promises given to the nation Israel. Premillennialism firmly holds that these are not in any sense transferred to the Church, which statement can be proved by showing that the Church in its entirety is never designated Israel in Scripture. If she were, then there would be good reason for transferring the promises which belong to Israel as well as the name.

The next logical step in the proof, then, is to show that a contrast is maintained in Scripture between Israel, the Gentiles,

[8] *Ibid.*, p. 33.

and the Church. This will be done by showing from the New Testament that (1) natural Israel and the Gentiles are contrasted, (2) natural Israel and the Church are contrasted, and (3) Jewish Christians are contrasted with Gentile Christians.

That natural Israel and the Gentiles are contrasted in the New Testament is seen from the fact that Israel is addressed as a nation after the Church has been established. Peter recognized this distinction, for he, "filled with the Holy Ghost, said unto them Ye rulers of the people, and elders of Israel" (Acts 4:8; *cf.* Acts 3:12a; 21:28; Rom. 10:1). It should be perfectly evident from these verses that natural Israel and Gentiles are contrasted in the New Testament.

The term *Jew* is also used in the New Testament after the institution of the Church. Paul says, "Give none offence, neither to the Jews, nor to the Gentiles, nor to the church of God" (1 Cor. 10:32). If the Jewish people were the same group as the Church or the Gentiles, then certainly there would be no point in the apostle's distinction in this passage.

Further, in Romans 9:4-5 Paul says concerning the nation Israel:

> Who are Israelites; to whom pertaineth the adoption, and the glory, and the covenants, and the giving of the law, and the service of God, and the promises; Whose are the fathers, and of whom as concerning the flesh Christ came, who is over all, God blessed for ever. Amen.

Paul is obviously referring to natural Israel for he calls them his "kinsmen according to the flesh" (verse 3), and it is to these people that he relates all these peculiar privileges. The fact that these words were spoken after the beginning of the Church is proof that the Church does not rob Israel of her blessings. Notice that Paul refers to the *covenants* which would be irrelevant if the covenants had been abrogated because of disobedience or unbelief. Israel's greatest act of unbelief had already occurred in her rejection of Christ. Further proof is found in Ephesians 2:12-15:

> That at that time ye were without Christ, being aliens from the commonwealth of Israel, and strangers from the covenants of promise, having no hope, and without God in the world: But now in Christ Jesus ye who sometimes were far off are made nigh by the blood of Christ. For he is our peace, who hath made both one, and hath broken down the middle wall of partition between us; Having abolished in his flesh the enmity, even the law of commandments contained in ordinances; for to make in himself of twain one new man, so making peace.

In this passage Gentiles are expressly said to be excluded from the blessings peculiar to Israel. In going on to state their blessings in the church, Paul does not say that once having believed, these Gentiles now come into the Israelite blessings, but rather that God has brought about a new thing, the new man in Christ Jesus.

It is evident, then, that:

> It may be concluded without further argument that the distinction between natural Israel and Gentiles is continued after the institution of the church—Israel is still a genuine Israel, and the Gentiles continue to fulfill their part. While this fact of Scriptures is more or less admitted even by the amillennialist, the significance is not adequately realized. The continuance of Israel and Gentiles as such is a strong argument against either one being dispossessed of their own place. Israel is not reduced to the bankruptcy of the Gentiles—to become "stran-

gers from the covenants of promise" (Eph. 2:12), and the distinction between the two groups is maintained on the same sharp lines as before the church was instituted.[9]

In the second place, natural Israel and the church are contrasted in the New Testament. Concerning the importance of this distinction the same writer says:

> The amillennial position fully agrees to this contrast, but in doing so, its supporters do not realize that the basis of their own argument is jeopardized. If natural Israel continues as an entity apart from the church with its own program and destiny, it becomes at once an interesting and vital argument against the transfer of Israel's promises to the church or their loss by any other means. The amillennialists are forced to a position which by its nature is untenable. They must admit the existence of natural Israel apart from the church because it is too evident that this is a fact of Scripture and history. They cannot admit any program for them or any possibility of a national future for them.[10]

This point may also be proved by referring to Paul's contrast between the Jews and the church in 1 Corinthians 10:32. However, the most important proof passage is Romans 11 where God's program for Israel is outlined. It would be illogical to apply this chapter to spiritual Israel, for as Shedd points out:

> He is speaking most commonly in this chapter, of the nation as a whole, out of which, he says, a part are spiritually elected, *so that the nation as a whole are not rejected* [italics mine]. It would be superfluous to assert and endeavor to prove that the spiritual people of God are not "thrust out entirely." [11]

---

[9] Walvoord, *Bibliotheca Sacra*, CI, 408.
[10] *Ibid.*, p. 409.
[11] *Commentary on Romans*, p. 329.

Paul asks in this chapter if God has cast away His people, that is, natural Israel. The answer is an emphatic *no,* for Paul himself and the remnant prove that God has not cast away His people whom He foreknew (verse 2). In verses 7 to 10, the rest of the nation, that is, the unbelieving part, is contrasted with this remnant, but that distinction cannot vitiate the irrevocable promises made to Abraham. It is true that this unbelieving part has been judicially hardened, but the hardening is not permanent. In the meantime their fall has brought riches to the Gentiles, for the gospel has come unto them. But, this being true, "how much more their [Israel's] fulness?" (verse 12). In other words, the fullness of blessing for Israel will be "much more," but since this is future it conclusively proves that Israel will have a future.

In verses 17 to 24, Paul introduces the figure of the olive tree. The apostle does not say that Israel *is* the olive tree; rather, the olive tree is the place of privilege. Israel was the first definite group to be called to this place, but because of unbelief she was set aside or broken off. Now the place of privilege is occupied by the Gentiles, but it is perfectly clear that Israel will again be grafted into the olive tree (verses 23, 24). What would be the point of all this argument if there were no contrast in the mind of Paul between Israel and the Church?

Not only do 1 Corinthians 10:32 and Romans 11 prove that natural Israel and the Church are contrasted, but the simple yet astounding fact that Israel has continued as a nation until this very day is strong additional evidence. Other nations have decayed or been assimilated by other groups, but the Jews continue as a recognizable group. How vividly this is seen in the establishment of the nation Israel in the land of Palestine, an event which should prove beyond all doubt to anyone that natural Israel is not the Church.

In the third place, Jewish Christians (spiritual Israel) and Gentile Christians are contrasted in the New Testament. This is the most important of the contrasts, for as Walvoord points out:

> The twofold origin of Jewish Christians and Gentile Christians is obvious to all. In the attempt to disfranchise Israel of her promises, however, it is claimed that the church composed of both Gentiles and Jews takes Israel's place of blessing completely. It is pointed out that there has always been an inner circle of Israelites who were the "true Israel" and that these were the genuine inheritors of the promises, not the nation as a whole. . . . Is the church ever identified with true or spiritual Israel, that is, are Gentile Christians ever included in the designation *Israel?* [12]

Two passages, properly explained, will provide proof of this contrast between Jewish and Gentile Christians. The first, Romans 9:6, "For they are not all Israel, which are of Israel," is often taken as proof that only spiritual Israel, that is, the Church, are those who inherit the promises, the rest of Israel being excluded. However, properly interpreted, this text supports the fact that Gentile Christians are never included in the designation *Israel*. In brief, it means that being an Israelite by natural birth does not assure one of the life and favor promised the true Israelite who approaches God by faith. The contrast, then, is not between those who inherit Abraham's promises and those who do not, but rather it is between the promises which belong to Israel according to the flesh, and those which belong

[12] *Bibliotheca Sacra*, CI, 411.

to the Israelite who enters into them by faith, which latter promises also belong to the Gentile believer who then becomes a child of Abraham by faith (Gal. 3:6). The passage intimates nothing concerning the relationship of Israel and the Church, but it draws sharply the distinction between believing Israelites and unbelieving Israelites as to their present blessings. Both groups still remain genuine Israelites, but the distinction is made with regard to their attitude toward Christ. Believing Israelites come into all the blessings of the Church in this age while unbelieving Israelites do not. However, when their blindness is lifted, they will again be grafted into the olive tree of privilege. Thus this passage does not in any way prove that Gentile Christians are called Israel. Rather it distinguishes believing Israelites in this age as a distinct group in the body of Christ.

The second passage involved is Galatians 6:15-16:

> For in Christ Jesus neither circumcision availeth any thing, nor uncircumcision, but a new creature. And as many as walk according to this rule, peace be upon them, and mercy, and upon the Israel of God.

In this passage the question is, who is the Israel of God? The amillennialist asserts that the Israel of God is the entire body which is the Church. If this could be sustained it would weaken the premillennial position considerably. However, the very opposite is the truth, for instead of identification there is distinction in this passage. The apostle is singling out believing Jews in this benediction pronounced upon the entire body of Christ which, of course, includes these Jews.

It is true that grammar is not definitive in this case as the και may be either explicative or simply copulative. If it were explicative it would be translated *even* and would support the amillennial interpretation; if copulative, it would be translated in the usual sense *and,* and would support the premillennial view. Actually an absolute decision cannot be made from the verse itself, but general usage would favor the recognition of two classes in this verse.

It is another indication that Gentile and Jewish believers are on the same level since the conjunction links coordinate parts of the sentence. The apostle is invoking blessing upon all who walk according to the rule of grace; then, lest there be any misunderstanding regarding his attitude, he singles out believing Israelites as a special group. Ellicott, the Greek scholar, agrees with this view and says:

> Still, as it is doubtful whether και is ever used by St Paul in so *marked* an explicative force as must be assigned . . . and as it seems still more doubtful whether Christians generally could be called "the *Israel* of God" . . . the simple copulative meaning seems most probable . . . St Paul includes all in his blessing, of whatever stock and kindred; and then, with his thoughts turning (as they ever did) to his own brethren after the flesh (Rom. ix. 3), he pauses to specify those who were once Israelites according to the flesh (1 Cor. x. 18), but now are the Israel of God . . . true spiritual children of Abraham.[13]

We may safely conclude that if these key passages do not identify Israel and the Church, as amillennialists claim, then no passage in the New Testament does. In every case, the term is used of the nation Israel or of the believing remnant which

[13] *St Paul's Epistle to the Galatians,* p. 139.

has become part of the body of Christ. In no case are the national promises to Israel destroyed. By these three contrasts, natural Israel and the Gentiles, natural Israel and the Church, spiritual Israel and the Church, it is clear that the Church in its entirety is never designated Israel in Scripture. Thus there is no basis for transferring to the Church the promises which belong to Israel.

Since the Church does not fulfill the promises of the Abrahamic covenant, Israel herself must fulfill them at a future date. Since only premillennialism has a place for a future fulfillment, it must be the correct system of interpretation. However, in order to make this discussion complete concerning the future fulfillment of the Abrahamic covenant, it is necessary to show that the Scriptures teach positively that Israel is the nation which will fulfill these promises. To do this evidence from two lines will be presented: (1) from passages which clearly teach that Israel will be restored; and (2) from passages which show that Israel will possess the land again, thus fulfilling the promises of the covenant.

If the promises of the Abrahamic covenant are unconditional, as has been shown, and if the Church does not fulfill these promises, then the only logical conclusion is that Israel will be restored in order to fulfill them. However, since some insist that the nation has been completely rejected by God, two passages of Scripture must be carefully examined.

The first one is Matthew 21:43: "Therefore say I unto you, The kingdom of God shall be taken from you, and given to a nation bringing forth the fruits thereof." This verse, which appears immediately after the parable of the householder, in which judgment is pronounced on Israel, would seem to teach the complete disinheritance of Israel from all her promises. However, an accurate interpretation of this verse must answer these questions: what will be taken away, from whom is it taken, and to whom is it given?

It is the kingdom of God that is taken from them. A full discussion of the kingdom of heaven and the kingdom of God will be given under the Davidic covenant, but suffice it to say at this point that the kingdom of God is the sphere of true faith in God. It is significant that Matthew, who is the only Gospel writer to use the term *kingdom of heaven,* uses the other phrase here, and this is certainly at the special direction of the Holy Spirit. Furthermore, the kingdom of God is not identified with the millennial kingdom; thus, the Lord is *not* saying that the blessings and promises concerning the millennium have been taken from Israel. The Lord is saying to these Jews that, because they had rejected Him, they could not enter the kingdom of God, for "except a man be born again, he cannot see the kingdom of God" (John 3:3).

From whom was the kingdom of God taken? It seems clear that the *you* refers to the generation to whom the Lord was speaking. This interpretation does not contradict any hermeneutical principle, and it is consistent with Romans 11:26.

To whom would the kingdom be given? By *application,* the "nation bringing forth the fruits thereof" may mean any generation which will turn to Christ; but in its strict *interpretation* it refers to the nation Israel when she shall turn to the Lord and be saved before entering the millennial kingdom. The emphasis in this passage is that the unbelieving scribes and Pharisees would not be saved because of their rejection of Christ. Gaebelein gives a good summary of the verse:

The Word of the Lord is emphatic and absolute; there is no hope for them. The nation to whom the Lord promises the Kingdom is not the Church. The Church is called the Body of Christ, the Bride of Christ, the Habitation of God by the Spirit, the Lamb's Wife, but never a nation. The nation is Israel still, but that believing remnant of the nation, living when the Lord comes.[14]

The second passage which shows conclusively that Israel will be restored is the passage which deals with her future salvation, Romans 11:26-27.

> And so all Israel shall be saved: as it is written, There shall come out of Sion the Deliverer, and shall turn away ungodliness from Jacob: For this is my covenant unto them, when I shall take away their sins.

This passage properly belongs to the discussion of the new covenant and will be included there. It may be said now, however, that careful exegetes agree that Israel means Israel in this passage. In this chapter Paul has been speaking of the setting aside of Israel as a nation, so it follows that the restoration of Israel is as a nation. Some amillennialists have endeavored to make Israel mean the Church because of the use of the word *Zion*, which they spiritualize to mean the Church. But Thayer, the Greek authority, silences these claims when he declares that Zion in this passage is "the entire city of Jerusalem itself." [15] This passage teaches, then, that all Israel, in contrast to the remnant being saved today, will be saved at the Second Coming of Christ. From these two passages it is clear that Israel has not been cast off but will be restored to the place of blessing in

[14] *The Gospel of Matthew*, II, 138.
[15] *A Greek-English Lexicon of the New Testament*, p. 576.

the future. Israel, because she has not been disinherited, will be in a position to fulfill the Abrahamic covenant.

The second line of evidence concerns Israel's possession of the land. It has been shown that Israel will be able to fulfill the Abrahamic covenant since she will be restored; now let us see whether or not she actually does. This will be done by testing the provision in the Abrahamic covenant concerning the unconditional promise of the possession of the land of Palestine. The boundaries of the land were given in very definite terms:

> In that day Jehovah made a covenant with Abram saying, Unto thy seed have I given this land, from the river of Egypt unto the great river, the river Euphrates: the Kenite, and the Kenizzite, and the Kadmonite, and the Hittite, and the Perizzite, and the Rephaim, and the Amorite, and the Canaanite, and the Girgashite, and the Jebusite. (Gen. 15:18-21)

Since it has been demonstrated that the Palestinian covenant, though it laid down conditions for enjoyment of the land, in no way forfeits the title to the land given to Abraham, and since Solomon did not fulfill the promise to Abraham, the boundaries of his kingdom not being equivalent to those described in the Abrahamic covenant, and since the Church does not fulfill these specifically Israelitish promises, it follows that we must either admit that the promise will have a future fulfillment or that God is not faithful to His Word. Its fulfillment in the future involves the continuance of the nation Israel.

It is recognized that Israel has been in dispersion at various times in her history, but these dispersions do not abrogate the promise of the permanent possession of the land since they were imposed as a penalty for sin. This is easily proved by noting that the prediction concerning the first dispersion into Egypt was given (Gen. 15:13-16) after the land was promised to Abraham (Gen. 13:15) and before the promise was re-affirmed (Gen. 15:18-21). The dispersion and regathering were brought about as promised. The second dispersion into Babylon was also accomplished and some, but not all, returned to the land. A representation of the whole nation was reassembled in the land. The third and last dispersion began in 70 A.D. and continues to the present day. Israel has not yet returned from this dispersion although the prophecies of her final regathering are manifold, which prophecies must be fulfilled if the Bible is the Word of God (*cf.* Deut. 30:3; Isa. 11:11-12; Ezek. 37:21; Amos 9:15). The literal interpretation of these passages makes it clear that these promises have not been fulfilled. For ex-ample, at no time have the Jews been gathered from the four corners of the earth (Isa. 11:12). Israel's regathering is surely future. It is also clear that the Church does not possess the land of Palestine or any land, for members of the body of Christ are pilgrims and strangers on this earth. In spite of dispersions, then, Israel will possess her land again.

By way of parenthesis, it may be added that the ever-increas-ing Zionist movement and the formation of the nation Israel are of no small import. While these things are not the fulfill-ment of the Abrahamic covenant, still they are significant in-dications to the premillennialist that God is working, and they are highly embarrassing to the amillennialist.

This concludes the discussion of the Abrahamic covenant. The two questions asked at the outset have been answered. Israel is promised permanent possession of the land and per-manent existence as a nation. This is based on the unconditional character of the covenant. Since the Church does not fulfill the national promises of the covenant, these promises await a future fulfillment by the nation Israel. Other Scriptures were cited to show that the Lord has promised a future restoration of the nation and a return to the land. Thus, the unconditional, partially-fulfilled Abrahamic covenant becomes an important plank in the solid basis for the premillennial faith.

Chapter 5

Its Basis in the
DAVIDIC COVENANT

The second important covenant upon which premillennialism is based is the covenant with David. While the Abrahamic covenant is not often ignored by interpreters of the Word, the Davidic usually receives the merest attention. This is a fundamental defect, for the main themes of the covenant, namely the throne, the King, and the kingdom, are vitally important to any professed system of truth. It is not enough to say that all the promises of the Davidic covenant have been fulfilled by Christ. What aspects of the covenant have been fulfilled, what aspects remain to be fulfilled, the question of literal or spiritual fulfillment, the relation of the covenant and the kingdom to this age and to the Church, and the future millennial reign of Christ must all be included in a complete discussion of the covenant. Without a proper understanding of the Davidic covenant, God's purposes concerning His own Son, His throne, His kingdom, and His church are a hopeless blur. Premillennialism is the only system of truth which can bring these things into focus.

I. THE ANALYSIS OF THE COVENANT

In these words God made His covenant with David:

> And when thy days be fulfilled, and thou shalt sleep with thy fathers, I will set up thy seed after thee, which shall proceed out of thy bowels, and I will establish his kingdom. He shall build an house for my name, and I will stablish the throne of his kingdom for ever. I will be his father, and he shall be my son. If he commit iniquity, I will chasten him with the rod of men, and with the stripes of the children of men: But my mercy shall not depart away from him as I took it from Saul, whom I put away before thee. And thine house and thy kingdom shall be established for ever before thee: thy throne shall be established for ever. (2 Sam. 7:12-16)

The background of the covenant is familiar. David desired to build a temple for the Lord to replace the temporary tent-like tabernacle. David himself lived in a house of cedar and it seemed only congruous to him that there be a more permanent building for the center of worship. But to Nathan the prophet was revealed that God had something far greater in mind for David. In this revelation, which we call the Davidic covenant, there are made certain promises to David and certain ones to his yet unborn son.

The promises of the covenant to David. God promised three things to David. First, he was to have a posterity. The covenant explicitly states that he would have a son and that David's house would be established forever. This clearly has reference to David's physical descendants, for David's line would always be the royal line. Secondly, David's throne was to be established forever. Thirdly, David's kingdom was also to be established forever. This has reference to the earthly, political kingdom over Israel.

The promises of the covenant to Solomon. To Solomon likewise were promised three things. First, he was promised that he would be the one to build the temple. Secondly, God promised that Solomon's throne would be established forever. It is important to notice that Solomon received no promise that his seed would sit on that throne forever. The promise was that David's seed would never be abolished, but no similar promise was given to Solomon. This fine point must be recognized in order to reconcile the provisions of the covenant with the historic fulfillment, for Solomon's line was cut off from sitting on the throne of David. Thirdly, chastisement was promised for disobedience, but the perpetuity of the covenant is nevertheless assured. The Word of God is perfectly plain concerning this, as already quoted. It seems as though God especially anticipated the amillennial argument that disobedience abrogates the covenant, and so He specifically says that it would not. History records that disobedience did bring punishment, but the covenant stands sure.

II. THE HISTORIC FULFILLMENT
OF THE COVENANT

It is only necessary to mention briefly that David had a son, that David's throne was established, that David's kingdom was established, that Solomon built the temple, that his throne was established, and that he was punished for disobedience. It is agreed by all conservatives that these things were established forever, for all recognize that Christ is the ultimate fulfiller of these promises. Luke 1:31-33 makes this clear:

> And behold, thou shalt conceive in thy womb, and bring forth a son, and shalt call his name Jesus. He shall be great, and shall be called the Son of the Most High: and the Lord God shall give unto him the throne of his father David: and he shall

reign over the house of Jacob for ever; and of his kingdom there shall be no end.

Premillennialists agree with amillennialists in recognizing that David's posterity had its consummation and eternal fulfillment in Jesus Christ, for only the eternal Son of God could fulfill these promises. However, the question of fulfillment not only consists in whether or not Christ fulfills the promises of the covenant, but also must include a discussion of when and how He fulfills them. In brief, the amillennialist answer is that Christ fulfills these promises in His present session at the right hand of God. The kingdom, therefore, is solely a spiritual one. The premillennialist answers that the fulfillment is yet future and will take place when Christ returns to the earth to set up and reign over a literal kingdom beginning in the millennium and continuing throughout all eternity. This is the teaching of the Old Testament passages which confirm the yet unfulfilled promises of the covenant, and it is the teaching of the New Testament even though the King was rejected. But before considering this, it is necessary to deal with one additional problem concerning the historic fulfillment of the covenant.

The question which must be answered is this: does the historic *partial* fulfillment (conceived of as partial from the premillennial contention that Christ is not now fulfilling the provisions of the covenant) disallow a future literal fulfillment? The chief difficulties which history brings up are three: (1) there has been no continuous development or continued authority of the political kingdom of David, (2) Israel's captivity and the downfall of the kingdom would seem to argue against a literal interpretation for a future fulfillment, and (3) the centuries which have passed since the first advent of Christ would seem to indicate that a literal fulfillment should not be expected. Negatively, it should be remembered that amillennialism has just as much difficulty as premillennialism with the first two problems since they have to do with events before the first coming of Christ. Positively, the premillennial position holds that the partial historic fulfillment in no way mitigates against the future fulfillment for these four reasons. First, the Old Testament prophets expected a literal fulfillment even during Israel's periods of great apostasy. Secondly, the covenant demands a literal interpretation which also means a future fulfillment. Thirdly, the New Testament teaches that the present mystery form of the kingdom in no way abrogates the future literal fulfillment. Fourthly, the very words of the covenant teach that, although Solomon be disobedient, the covenant would nevertheless remain in force, and that Solomon's seed was not promised perpetuity. The only necessary feature is that the lineage cannot be lost, *not that the throne be occupied continuously*. It is a fact of history that Solomon's line was cut off from the throne (Jer. 22:30; 36:30), and although Joseph, Christ's legal father, was descended from Solomon (Matt. 1:7), Mary, His actual mother, was a descendant of another son of David, Nathan (Luke 3:31). The important conclusion from all this is that:

> . . . the line which was to fulfill the promise of the eternal throne and eternal kingdom over Israel was preserved by God through a lineage which in fact did not sit on the throne at all, from Nathan down to Christ. It is, then, not necessary for the line to be unbroken as to actual conduct of the kingdom, but it is rather that the lineage, royal prerogative, and right

to the throne be preserved and *never lost,* even in sin, captivity, and dispersion. It is not necessary, then, for continuous political government to be in effect, but *it is necessary that the line be not lost.*[1]

Part of the covenant, then, has been fulfilled literally in the past. That there have been and are interruptions in the carrying out of the provisions of the covenant does not mean that the yet unfulfilled parts will not be fulfilled in the future.

III. THE LITERAL INTERPRETATION OF THE COVENANT

The importance of literal interpretation. Only literal interpretation will bring out all the significantly prophetic features of the Davidic covenant. First of all, if the covenant is interpreted literally, then it follows that what Christ is doing now in His present session is not fulfilling the Davidic covenant. In the Old Testament the throne of David as perpetually promised is the throne of the house of Israel (Jer. 33:17). If Christ is the Man who is fulfilling Jeremiah's statement, then He is certainly not now fulfilling the Davidic covenant, for not one New Testament reference can be found which teaches that the Lord Jesus Christ is now on the throne of David, and His present relation to the Church certainly has no equivalence to the throne of the house of Israel. Twenty-one times in the New Testament Christ's present position is described by the phrase, "at the right hand" of God, or of the Majesty on High, etc., and this location is expressly defined as the throne of the Father (Rev. 3:21; 12:5).

[1] Walvoord, *Bibliotheca Sacra,* CII, 161.

It then follows that if Christ is not now fulfilling the Davidic covenant, there must be a future fulfillment, and if there is to be a future fulfillment, then the premillennial system of interpretation is required, for it alone gives a place for such a future earthly reign of Christ. Therefore, the question of literal interpretation is extremely important.

The arguments for literal interpretation. There is no better list of arguments for the literal interpretation of the Davidic covenant than the one which Peters gives.

(1) It is *solemnly covenanted, confirmed by oath,* and hence cannot be altered or broken.

(2) The grammatical sense *alone is becoming* a covenant.

(3) The impression made on David, if erroneous, is *disparaging* to his prophetical office.

(4) The conviction of Solomon (2 Chron. 6:14-16) was that *it referred* to the literal throne and Kingdom.

(5) Solomon claims that the covenant was fulfilled in himself, but *only in so far* that he too as David's son sat on David's throne. Some from this wrongfully infer that the entire promise is conditional over against *the most express declarations to the contrary* as to the distinguished One, the pre-eminent Seed. It was indeed, conditional as to the ordinary seed of David . . . and if his seed would have yielded obedience, David's throne would *never* have been vacated until the Seed, par excellence, came. . . . The reader will not fail to observe that if fulfilled in Solomon, and not having respect unto the Seed, how incongruous and irrelevant would be the prophecies *given afterward,* as e. g. Jer. 33:17-26, etc.

(6) The language is that *ordinarily used* to denote *the literal* throne and Kingdom of David. . . .

(7) The prophets adopt the *same language,* and its *constant reiteration* under Divine guidance is evidence that the plain grammatical sense is the one intended.

(8) The prevailing belief of centuries, a national faith, *en-*

gendered by the language, under the teaching of inspired men, indicates *how* the language is to be understood.

(9) This throne and Kingdom is one of promise and inheritance, and hence refers not to the Divinity but *to the Humanity* of Jesus.

(10) This same is distinctively promised to David's Son *"according to the flesh"* to be actually realized, and, therefore, He must appear the Theocratic King as promised.

(11) We have not the slightest hint given that it is to be interpreted in any other way than a literal one; any other is the result of *pure inference.*

(12) Any other view than that of a literal interpretation involves the grossest *self-contradiction.*

(13) The denial of a literal reception of the covenant *robs the heir* of His covenanted inheritance.

(14) No grammatical rule *can* be laid down which will make David's throne to be the Father's throne in the third heaven.

(15) That if the latter is attempted under the notion of "symbolical" or "typical," then the credibility and meaning of the covenants are *left to the interpretations of men,* and David himself becomes the "symbol" or "type" of the Creator.

(16) That if David's throne is the Father's throne in heaven, *then* it must have existed forever.

(17) If such covenanted promises are to be received figuratively, it is inconceivable that they should be given in their present form without some *direct affirmation,* in some place, of their figurative nature, God foreseeing (if not literal) that for centuries they would be pre-eminently calculated to foster false expectations, e. g. even from David to Christ.

(18) God is faithful in His promises and *deceives no one* in the language of His covenants.

(19) No necessity existed, why if this throne promised to David's Son meant something else, the throne *should be so definitely promised* in the form given.

(20) The *identical* throne and Kingdom overthrown are the ones restored.

(21) . . . These, in connection with the covenants themselves, make David's throne and Kingdom a requisite for the

display of that *Theocratic* ordering which God has already instituted . . . for the restoration and exaltation of the Jewish
nation . . . for the salvation of the human race . . . and for
the dominion of a renewed curse-delivered world. . . . Such a
throne and Kingdom *are necessary to preserve the Divine Unity
of Purpose in the already proposed Theocratic line.*[2]

These reasons conclusively prove that the only proper way
to regard the covenant is literally, and this being true, the
covenant must have a future fulfillment which is according to
the premillennial system of interpretation.

IV. THE CONFIRMATION OF THE COVENANT
IN THE OLD TESTAMENT

The Old Testament is replete with confirmations of the promise of God to establish His kingdom on the earth. The prophets
are united in their testimony, looking forward to and proclaim-
ing a Messiah who would establish the house of David on
David's throne over David's kingdom. No other conclusion is
possible without perverting the meaning of these prophecies.

In the Psalms. Brief mention should be made of the forty-
fifth Psalm which speaks of the marriage of the King and of
the seventy-second Psalm which speaks of His character. By
no stretch of the imagination could this be made to refer to
Solomon. The principal confirming Psalm is the eighty-ninth
which says in part:

I have made a covenant with my chosen, I have sworn unto
David my servant, Thy seed will I establish for ever, and build

[2] *Op. cit.,* 1, 343-44.

up thy throne to all generations. . . . My mercy will I keep for him for evermore, and my covenant shall stand fast with him, His seed also will I make to endure for ever, and his throne as the days of heaven. If his children forsake my law, and walk not in my judgments; If they break my statutes, and keep not my commandments; Then will I visit their transgression with the rod, and their iniquity with stripes. Nevertheless my lovingkindness will I not utterly take from him, nor suffer my faithfulness to fail. My covenant will I not break, nor alter the thing that is gone out of my lips. Once have I sworn by my holiness that I will not lie unto David. His seed shall endure for ever, and his throne as the sun before me. It shall be established for ever as the moon, and as a faithful witness in heaven. (Verses 3, 4, 28-37)

The Lord seemed to anticipate the amillennial argument, but He clearly and definitely says that He will not alter or spiritualize, if you please, the thing that has gone out of His lips (*cf.* verse 34). Surely there could be no more certain confirmation of the future King and kingdom than this which was given to David.

In Isaiah. Isaiah, a contemporary of Micah, also prophesied concerning the visible, earthly kingdom as promised in the Davidic covenant. In the days of the approaching Assyrian invasion, he said:

For unto us a child is born, unto us a son is given: and the government shall be upon his shoulder: and his name shall be called Wonderful, Counsellor, The mighty God, The everlasting Father, The Prince of Peace. Of the increase of his government and peace there shall be no end, upon the throne of David, and upon his kingdom, to order it, and to establish it with judgment and with justice from henceforth even for ever. The zeal of the Lord of hosts will perform this. (Isa. 9:6-7)

Chapters 11, 24, 25, 54, 60, 61, etc., all describe various aspects of the kingdom and add to the proof that the kingdom promised to David and confirmed by Isaiah is not the present session of Christ in heaven. Of course, this is based on a literal interpretation of these passages, but this only further confirms the consistency of the premillennial position.

In Jeremiah. Jeremiah standing among the falling ruins of the kingdom nevertheless had the same unchanging confidence in the covenant that was made with David. In the chapter immediately following the prediction of the cutting off of Solomon's line from the throne, Jeremiah says:

> Behold, the days come, saith the Lord, that I will raise unto David a righteous Branch, and a King shall reign and prosper, and shall execute judgment and justice in the earth. In his days Judah shall be saved, and Israel shall dwell safely: and this is his name whereby he shall be called, THE LORD OUR RIGHTEOUSNESS. (23:5-6)

Certainly there was no fulfillment of this promise in the first advent of the Man of sorrows. The world still awaits the day when this glorious King shall reign and prosper *in the earth*.

Again the prophet speaks:

> For it shall come to pass in that day, saith the Lord of hosts, that I will break his yoke from off thy neck, and will burst thy bonds, and strangers shall no more serve themselves of him: But they shall serve the Lord their God, and David their king, whom I will raise up unto them. (30:8-9)

> Behold, the days come, saith the Lord, that I will perform that good thing which I have promised unto the house of Israel and to the house of Judah. In those days, and at that time, will I cause the Branch of righteousness to grow up unto David;

and he shall execute judgment and righteousness in the land. In
those days shall Judah be saved, and Jerusalem shall dwell
safely: and this is the name wherewith she shall be called The
Lord our righteousness. For thus saith the Lord; David shall
never want a man to sit upon the throne of the house of
Israel. . . . Thus saith the Lord; If ye can break my covenant
of the day, and my covenant of the night, and that there
should not be day and night in their season; Then may also
my covenant be broken with David my servant. (33:14-17,
20-21)

If the prophet meant what he said—and what else can we
believe?—nothing from human history since the days of the
Babylonian captivity can be produced in fulfillment of these
words.

In Ezekiel. Ezekiel, a prophet of the exile, speaks in the same
manner of the coming kingdom.

And David my servant shall be king over them; and they all
shall have one shepherd: they shall also walk in my judgments,
and observe my statutes, and do them. And they shall dwell
in the land that I have given unto Jacob my servant, wherein
your fathers have dwelt; and they shall dwell therein, even
they, and their children, and their children's children for ever:
and my servant David shall be their prince for ever. (37:24-25)

In Daniel. Daniel, also a prophet of the exile, is important,
for he fixes the time of the kingdom as at the Second, not the
first, Advent of the Lord Jesus. In the prophecy recorded in
Daniel 7:13-14, he says:

I saw in the night visions, and, behold, one like the Son of
man came with the clouds of heaven, and came to the Ancient
of days, and they brought him near before him. And there was
given him dominion, and glory, and a kingdom, that all people,

nations, and languages, should serve him: his dominion is an everlasting dominion, which shall not pass away, and his kingdom that which shall not be destroyed.

In the minor prophets. In the so-called minor prophets there are a number of passages which speak of the Davidic kingdom. We can only notice a few of them.

Hosea anticipates Israel's separation from their right relationship with God, but he also foretells with equal certainty their return.

> For the children of Israel shall abide many days without a king, and without a prince, and without a sacrifice, and without an image, and without an ephod, and without teraphim: Afterward shall the children of Israel return, and seek the Lord their God, and David their king; and shall fear the Lord and his goodness in the latter days. (3:4-5)

Amos speaks of the same event when he says:

> In that day will I raise up the tabernacle of David that is fallen, and close up the breaches thereof; and I will raise up his ruins, and I will build it as in the days of old. (9:11)

Zechariah declares that at Christ's second coming, when "his feet shall stand . . . upon the mount of Olives" (14:4), "the Lord shall be king over all the earth" (14:9). This, like Daniel's prophecy, fixes the time of the kingdom as beginning at the Second Advent of Christ.

Thus the Old Testament proclaims a kingdom to be established on the earth by the Messiah, the Son of David, as heir of the Davidic covenant. The Jews expected such a kingdom for they took God literally at His word, which strongly and repeatedly confirmed the hopes and promises of the covenant with David.

V. THE CONFIRMATION OF THE COVENANT IN THE NEW TESTAMENT

There is little doubt that the Old Testament predicted an earthly kingdom. The all-important question is, did Christ change in any way this conception when He came to earth and was rejected by His own people? In order to answer fully this question it will be necessary to show the nature of the kingdom as it was anticipated by the Jews from their own concept of that kingdom and from the preaching of the day. Then the rejection, mystery form, and future real form of the kingdom must be examined from the Scriptures, for this is the crux of the matter and the chief point of disagreement between premillennialism and amillennialism.

In the Jews' concept of the kingdom at the time of Christ. In spite of the degraded political and moral condition of the nation Israel at the time of Christ, the national hope of a kingdom was exceedingly strong. Jewish thought at that time was permeated with the thought of this kingdom. The terms, kingdom of God, kingdom of heaven, etc., were on everyone's lips. The concept which the Jews had of this kingdom at this time may be summed up under these five characteristics: earthly, national, Messianic, moral, and future.[3]

The hope was for an earthly kingdom. When Israel saw Palestine under the rule of a foreign power, her hope was the

[3] Ceperley, *The Kingdom Concept at the Time of Christ and Its Significance,* pp. 13-19.

more intensified, because the kingdom she expected was one
that would be set up on the earth and one that would naturally
carry with it release from foreign domination. The Scripture
bears testimony to this for repeatedly Christ is spoken of as
"He that should come" (Luke 7:19), of the One whom the
people wanted to crown as king (John 6:15). The nation conceived of a kingdom to be set up on the earth (*cf.* Matt. 20:20;
Luke 1:71; 19:17; 24:21).

The kingdom was to be national; that is, the expected kingdom had a specific relationship to Israel, being promised to
that nation alone. Other nations were not to be left outside the
blessings of the kingdom, but it was to center in Israel with
Jerusalem as its capital.

The expected kingdom has often been referred to as the Messianic kingdom since Messiah was to reign. Because of the
nature of the expected kingdom, the Messiah who was to come
took on the character of a great deliverer and military leader
in the minds of the Jews of that day. Since they recognized
that He was to be born in Bethlehem, they thought He was
to live first in concealment before coming forth as a deliverer.

The kingdom was to be a moral kingdom, for Israel was to
be cleansed as a nation. However, the nation longed so for the
deliverance from political oppression that little thought was
given to turning from sin. This is why the preaching of repentance as a condition of entrance into the kingdom was such
a stumbling block to the people.

Obviously the kingdom was not yet in existence and was
therefore future at the time of the first coming of the Lord
Jesus Christ. Even all the glory under David and Solomon was
not comparable to the expected kingdom. Consequently, all of

Israel's beliefs concerning this kingdom were of the nature of unrealized hopes. Israel looked to the future.

In this fivefold characterization of the Jews' expectation of the kingdom there is definite confirmation of the features of the Davidic covenant.

In the preaching of John the Baptist. John the Baptist's message was simplicity itself. Matthew has recorded it: "In those days came John the Baptist, preaching in the wilderness of Judea, And saying, Repent ye: for the kingdom of heaven is at hand" (Matt. 3:1-2). It is important to notice that the word kingdom as used by John in his preaching is always made definite by the use of the article. John does not speak of *a* kingdom but *the* kingdom, and as far as the record is concerned it is the kingdom of heaven. John also preached that it was *at hand;* that is, that it was future and next on God's program for the Jewish nation. John does not define the nature of the kingdom which he preached; rather, his exhortation was to repent of sin. But in all of his preaching he confirms the hopes contained in the promises of the Davidic covenant.

In the preaching of Christ. The ministry of the Lord Jesus Christ was directed at first to the nation Israel. At His birth it was announced that "he shall save his people from their sins" (Matt. 1:21), and the wise men sought the "King of the Jews" (Matt. 2:2) who would rule the people Israel. Christ continued to preach the message of the kingdom where John left off, for "from that time Jesus began to preach, and to say, Repent: for the kingdom of heaven is at hand" (Matt. 4:17, *cf.* 4:23; 9:35). The terminology is identical with that of John the Baptist, for it is *the* kingdom of which Christ spoke and it is viewed as being at hand.

In addition, the kingdom which Christ preached was one of righteousness. Entrance was to be based on religious profession, the righteousness of which was to exceed that of the scribes and Pharisees (Matt. 5:20). The Lord elaborates on the moral requirements in the Sermon on the Mount which is a manifesto of the kingdom and which would have been put into effect immediately had the offer of the kingdom been accepted at that time. All the conditions were right—the King was there present, the offer of the kingdom had been made, great multitudes were following Him (Matt. 4:25). And so the King presents the constitution of the kingdom in the Sermon on the Mount, but it was the very high standard of morality that would be required that the Jews refused to accept.

In the preaching of the twelve. The twelve disciples were the first commissioned by the Lord to proclaim the kingdom message.

> These twelve Jesus sent forth, and commanded them, saying, Go not into the way of the Gentiles, and into any city of the Samaritans enter ye not. But go rather to the lost sheep of the house of Israel. And as ye go, preach, saying, The kingdom of heaven is at hand. (Matt. 10:5-7)

Two things from this passage are striking. First, the message was the same as that preached by John the Baptist and by Christ. Secondly, the witness was to be only to the nation Israel. The twelve are specifically commanded not to go to the Gentiles or even to the Samaritans. How can this be explained except as a confirmation of the Davidic covenant?

All the evidence points to the confirmation of the visible, earthly kingdom as first promised to David. This was the kingdom announced by John the Baptist. It was the content of the early ministry of Christ and of the twelve disciples whom He commissioned.

In the mystery form of the kingdom. This is the crucial point in the interpretation of the Davidic covenant. The kingdom of heaven (literally *of* the heavens, not *in* the heavens) which Christ faithfully offered while on earth was the very same earthly, Messianic, Davidic kingdom which the Jews expected from the Old Testament prophecies. But it is a matter of history that such a kingdom was not ushered in at the first advent of Christ. Does this abrogate the covenant, or was something new introduced at that time? In the understanding of the mystery form of the kingdom lies the answer. Two things enter into this: the rejection of the offered kingdom, and the Lord's actual teaching concerning the mystery form of the kingdom.

Evidence of the rejection of the kingdom is found in many places. The first is seen in the record that John the Baptist was placed in prison (Matt. 11:2). Because of this rejection of John as well as the rejection of His own message (*cf.* verse 19), the Lord Jesus pronounces judgment on the cities wherein He had given greatest proof of His messiahship through the miracles He had performed (Matt. 11:20-21). (It is significant that at the end of this chapter, in which occurs this first evidence of the rejection of the kingdom, these words appear: "Come unto me, all ye that labour and are heavy laden, and I will give you rest" (verse 28), for these are words which are entirely foreign to the kingdom message.) In chapter twelve the record of the unpardonable sin is given, and these two chapters seem to be the turning point in the account. Nevertheless, other evidences of Christ's rejection are seen even to the very end of His life. Later on in His ministry this occurred:

> When Jesus came into the coasts of Caesarea Philippi, he asked his disciples, saying, Whom do men say that I the Son of man am? And they said, Some say that thou art John the Baptist: some, Elias; and others, Jeremias, or one of the prophets. (Matt. 16:13-14)

Near the very end of His life, Christ is seen still offering Himself to the nation as their King, riding meek and lowly into Jerusalem (Matt. 21), that the Scriptures might be fulfilled. At the very end He dies under the claim to be the King of the Jews (Matt. 27:37). Clearly, then, the kingdom was rejected by Israel.

The second part of the discussion concerns the teaching by our Lord of the mystery form of the kingdom, and the principal passage involved is Matthew 13. Though the details of this chapter have been a battleground for interpreters through the years, it is only within our purpose to consider certain features which are vital to the doctrine of the kingdom. Each of the seven parables in the chapter, except the first one, is introduced with the phrase "the kingdom of heaven is like to." However, in explaining to the disciples the meaning of the first parable, which Christ had not introduced in that way, He told them that to them it was given "to know the mysteries of the kingdom of heaven" (verse 11). The subject, then, is well-established.

It is important to notice the time limits in the passage. The second parable is introduced by these words, literally, "The kingdom of the heavens has become like unto." This sets the time limit for the *beginning* of the subject matter involved. In other words, the kingdom of heaven was assuming the form described in the parables at that time when Christ was personally ministering on the earth. The *end* of the time period covered by these parables is indicated by the phrase "end of the world" or more literally "the consummation of the age" (verses 39-49). This is the time of the Second Advent of Christ when He shall come in power and great glory. Therefore, it is clear that these parables are concerned only with that time between the days when Christ spoke them on the earth and the end of this age. This gives a clue to the meaning of the phrase "the mysteries of the kingdom of heaven."

Certainly the kingdom was not set up when Christ was on earth. Instead it was rejected. However, the kingdom of heaven in mystery form was established at the first advent of Christ. A mystery in the Scriptures is a truth previously hidden but finally revealed. This is the definition usually accepted by premillennialists and will have to be assumed to be correct at this point. It will be defended by an inductive study in the chapter on ecclesiology. In Matthew 13 the Lord is introducing the mysteries of the kingdom, that is, something that was formerly unknown but which is now revealed. The kingdom itself was not unknown to the Old Testament prophets as has been shown, but the mystery form of the kingdom was unknown then and could not be known until Christ's genuine offer of the kingdom had been rejected. It is the mystery form of the kingdom of which the Lord speaks in this chapter, and this is the form in which the kingdom is established in this present age.

This is all-important for it shows ultimately that the present session of Christ is not the fulfillment of the Davidic covenant. If it were, then the Lord need not have introduced the mystery form of the kingdom at all, but rather He should have told the disciples that He would fulfill the Davidic covenant in a new way, that is, by His session in heaven. He did introduce something new, but it was not, as the amillennialist claims, His present session in heaven, but instead it was the mystery form of the kingdom. This coupled with the fact that the real form of the kingdom, that is, the earthly, Messianic, and national kingdom, was spoken of after this mystery form was introduced confirms the premillennial interpretation of the New Testament confirmations of the Davidic covenant.

While it is impossible to give here a detailed interpretation of each of these parables, certain characteristic features of the kingdom of heaven must be noticed. In doing so, the contrast between these and the characteristics of the Church will be evident, and all of this will add to the proof that the Church is not the kingdom over which Christ is now reigning.

The parable of the sower teaches that religious profession is a characteristic of the mystery form of the kingdom of heaven. Those who hear the word of the Sower and who consequently make some sort of religious profession are themselves then cast into the world for a testimony (*cf.* the phrase "he that was sown" in verses 19, 20, 22, 23, R. V.). Only one-fourth of them bear fruit, some to a greater and some to a lesser degree. This one-fourth seem to be the only ones who are truly saved, for the point of the parable is that profession is characteristic of the kingdom.

The second parable, the wheat and the tares, teaches the presence of counterfeits in the kingdom of heaven, a characteristic certainly not true of the Church. These are unquestionably unbelievers, for they are called by the Lord "children of the wicked one" (verse 38). That they are in the kingdom of heaven is also without question, for they are "among the wheat" (verse 25).

The parable of the mustard seed teaches the abnormal growth of the mystery form of the kingdom. The birds of the air (verses 4, 19, *cf.* Rev. 18:2) which lodge in the branches represent demonized human beings who are part of Christendom. Abnormal growth and the sheltering of false religions, then, are the two characteristics of the kingdom taught in this parable.

Leaven always speaks of evil, but not necessarily of evil persons. Here, in this fourth parable, it may refer to evil doctrine which shall permeate the kingdom of heaven in its mystery form. If evil persons were meant, this parable would teach the same truth as the second one—a seemingly needless repetition. Evil doctrine, according to this parable, is characteristic of the kingdom.

The parable of the treasure speaks of the inclusion of Israel in the kingdom of heaven, for Israel is yet to be restored and saved. This takes place at the very end of the mystery form of the kingdom (Matt. 22:1-10).

The parable of the pearl teaches that the Church, the body of Christ, is also a part of the kingdom of heaven in its mystery form. This was also taught in the first and second parables.

The last parable, the dragnet, brings out the truth that the unbelieving element of the kingdom will be separated from the believing element at the end of the mystery form of the kingdom.

From this brief discussion of Matthew 13, two facts stand out as being especially important to the argument. First, the characteristics of the kingdom preclude its being the Church, which in turn means that the Church is not fulfilling the Davidic covenant, and, secondly, the form of the kingdom in this present age is temporary.

Before showing that the real form of the kingdom is also promised in the New Testament, a brief word concerning the relation of the terms *kingdom of heaven* and *kingdom of God* would be in place, although not absolutely vital to the argument, since amillennialists have seized upon this distinction with seemingly great glee, calling it "hairsplitting." If we believe that the very words of the Scripture are inspired, then we must believe that these different terms are not used by accident or without purpose. Further, this brief discussion should serve to show that premillennialism is the only system of interpretation which can cope with such distinctions.

The phrase *kingdom of heaven* which is used at least thirty-six times is confined to Matthew's Gospel. The phrase *kingdom of God* is used explicitly at least seventy-two times in the New Testament. The characteristics of the two are different. The kingdom of heaven is characterized by religious profession; the kingdom of God, by the new birth (John 3:3). It follows that there are no unbelievers in the kingdom of God, and nowhere is a separation of unbelievers out of the kingdom of God spoken of. Both the kingdom of heaven and the kingdom of God experience abnormal growth in the world (Mark 4:30-32), and both include a saved remnant of Israel and the Church. In brief, there are significant distinctions between the two that make it erroneous to equate the terms; on the other hand, the similarities pose no contradictions.

Exactly parallel passages in the Synoptic Gospels, which would seem to make the kingdom of heaven and kingdom of God equivalent terms, are: Matthew 4:17 and Mark 1:15; Matthew 10:7 and Luke 9:2; Matthew 11:11 and Luke 7:28; Matthew 13:11, Mark 4:11 and Luke 8:10; and Matthew 13:31 and Mark 4:20. However, we still must insist that similarity is not equivalence and that the distinctions are not contradicted. In addition, it should be remembered, in considering this entire problem, that the Holy Spirit may quote Himself in the different Gospel accounts with complete freedom; that Christ's messages were delivered in Aramaic and translated into Greek after being condensed and interpreted under the guidance of the Holy Spirit; that God led the various writers to select from the sayings of Christ those things which were in keeping with the theme of each particular book; and in each of the five instances listed above, what is said of the kingdom of heaven and the kingdom of God is true of both.

In the real form of the kingdom. When the Lord Jesus Christ introduced the truth of the mystery form of the kingdom, did He abrogate all the promises of the Davidic covenant for the earthly, national, Messianic, moral, and future kingdom? The answer is an emphatic *no,* and this will be proved by citing three passages which concern the real form of the kingdom but which were spoken *after* the time at which the Lord introduced the truth of the mystery form of the kingdom.

The first is the parable of the ten virgins (Matt. 25:1-13). Like the parables of Matthew 13 this one has been variously misinterpreted, but for the present discussion our chief interest in the parable is to determine the time indicated by it. If it refers to the Second Coming of Christ, then this is proof that the promises concerning the kingdom in its real form as anticipated by the Jews and proclaimed by John the Baptist and others have not been abrogated, for this is a parable of the kingdom of heaven (verse 1). Considering the entire Olivet discourse in which this parable is set, it is evident, even without a detailed exposition of all the words and phrases in the discourse which have a time element in them, that all of them refer to the great tribulation or to events connected with the Second Coming of Christ (*cf.* Matt. 24:3, 6, 7, 14, 15, 21, 29, 30, 37, 42, 44; 25:10, 19, 31). If the discourse as a whole refers to the times of the Second Advent then the parable of the ten virgins must also be interpreted of the last times of Israel. One agrees with Andrus who says that a consistent interpretation of the parable itself would be that:

> The Bridegroom is coming *with* the bride to a wedding feast on the earth (in the first part of the kingdom of heaven, the millennial kingdom of Christ). . . . The virgins of the parable are not waiting with the bride but as a welcoming party waiting for the Bridegroom and the bride.[4]

Whether or not one agrees with all the details of such an interpretation, the fact still remains that the kingdom of heaven is linked with the Second Coming of Christ and is not abrogated by the present mystery form.

The Lord Jesus also confirms Israel's hope for an earthly kingdom in His teaching concerning the judgment of the na-

---

[4] *The Parable of the Ten Virgins*, p. 43.

tions (Matt. 25:31-46). Without going into all the details of
the interpretation of the passage, one would point out that to
the nations on the right hand Christ says, "Come, ye blessed
of my Father, inherit the kingdom prepared for you from the
foundation of the world" (verse 34). Fundamentally, it makes
relatively little difference whether the judgment is national or
individual, whether unsaved individuals enter the millennium
or not, or what is the place of Gentiles (with whom this judgment is concerned) in the kingdom.[5] Not one of these alternate
views would weaken the proof intended from this passage; that
is, that the Lord, even after announcing the mystery form of
the kingdom, teaches that there is a future real form which
will be ushered in at His Second Coming.

The last passage to be cited as proof that the real form of
the kingdom has not been abrogated is the Amos quotation in
Acts 15:14-17. While it has been shown that on the basis of
literal interpretation of Luke 1:31-33 it is God's purpose to
fulfill the Davidic covenant, that there is not one reference con-
necting the present session of Christ with the Davidic throne,
that the kingdom is in mystery form today, that the real form
is still expected in the future, a proper understanding of this
passage will clinch the argument that the present work of
Christ is not identical with the future kingdom reign. The
council had met in Jerusalem to face the question of the relationship of Judaism to Christianity. Schaff has well said that:

> The question of circumcision, or of the terms of admission of
> the Gentiles to the Christian church . . . involved the wider

---

[5] *Cf.* Hamilton, *op. cit.*, pp. 70-78, who makes much of these minor points in
order to cloud the real issue.

question of the binding authority of the Mosaic law, yea, the whole relation of Christianity to Judaism.[6]

After private and public deliberations, the key speech was delivered by James who said:

> Simeon hath declared how God at the first did visit the Gentiles, to take out of them a people for his name. And to this agree the words of the prophets; as it is written, After this I will return, and will build again the tabernacle of David, which is fallen down; and I will build again the ruins thereof, and I will set it up: That the residue of men might seek after the Lord, and all the Gentiles, upon whom my name is called, saith the Lord, who doeth all these things (Acts 15:14-17).

The entire ninth chapter of Amos from which the quotation is taken bears on the interpretation of these verses in Acts, for Amos confirms the fact that the "tabernacle of David" is the nation of Israel in contrast to the Gentile nations. No exegesis could make it equivalent to the New Testament Church. Gaebelein gives a good analysis of James' words citing four points in the progression of thought.[7] First, God visits the Gentiles, taking from them a people for His name. In other words, God has promised to bless the Gentiles as well as Israel, but each in his own order. The Gentile blessing is first. Secondly, Christ will return. This is *after* the outcalling of the people for His name. Thirdly, as a result of the Coming of the Lord, the tabernacle of David will be built again; that is, the kingdom will be established as promised in the Davidic covenant. Amos clearly declares that this rebuilding will be done "as in the days of old" (9:11); that is, the blessings will be earthly and

---

[6] *Op. cit.*, I, 335.
[7] *The Acts of the Apostles*, pp. 265-69.

national and will have nothing to do with the Church. Fourthly, the residue of men will seek the Lord, that is, all the Gentiles will be brought to a knowledge of the Lord after the kingdom is established. Isaiah 2:2; 11:10; 40:5; 66:23 teach the same truth. Summarizing the teaching of these verses Walvoord has well said:

> Instead of identifying the period of Gentile conversion with the rebuilding of the tabernacle of David, it is carefully distinguished by the *first* (Gentile blessing), and *after this*, referring to Israel's coming glory. The passage instead of identifying God's purpose for the church and for the nation Israel established a specific time order. Israel's blessing will not come until "I return," apparently a reference to the second coming of Christ. That it could not refer either to the Incarnation or to the coming of the Spirit at Pentecost is evident in that neither are "return's." The passage under consideration constitutes, then, an important guide in determining the purpose of God. God will first conclude His work for the Gentiles in the period of Israel's dispersion; then He will return to bring in the promised blessings for Israel. It is needless to say that this confirms the interpretation that Christ is not now on the throne of David bringing blessing to Israel as the prophets predicted, but He is rather on His Father's throne waiting for the coming earthly kingdom and interceding for His own who form the church.[8]

This concludes the study of the Davidic covenant. It has been shown that the covenant demands literal interpretation and literal fulfillment. Some of its promises have been fulfilled, but this in no way hinders a future fulfillment; in fact, it guarantees it. The covenant was confirmed over and over in the Old Testament, all the prophets agreeing as to the literal, future, earthly kingdom. Moreover, the New Testament does

[8] *Bibliotheca Sacra,* CII, 164.

not in any way abrogate the provisions of the covenant. It is true that a new thing is revealed; that is, the mystery form of the kingdom, but explicit references to the kingdom as promised and anticipated in the Old Testament are also found after the revelation of the mystery form of the kingdom. Finally, the New Testament nowhere identifies the present work of Christ with the throne and kingdom of David, but rather specifically separates the period of present Gentile blessing from that of Israel's future glory. Thus, in the Davidic covenant premillennialism has a firm basis.

Chapter 6

Its Basis in the
NEW COVENANT

Although the new covenant is one of the major covenants of Scripture, a clear statement of its meaning and of its relation to the premillennial system is needed. Even among premillennialists there seems to be a lack of knowledge concerning this covenant.

As in the other covenants, the question here is again the question of fulfillment. No matter what may be the eschatological persuasion, all conservatives recognize that God made a promise of a new covenant when He said, "I will make a new covenant with the house of Israel, and with the house of Judah" (Jer. 31:31), and all agree that our God keeps His word. While admitting this, however, many do not face fairly the question of fulfillment.

It is of utmost importance in treating this subject to compare the Old Testament and the New Testament teaching concerning the new covenant with Israel. If, as some claim, the New Testament alters the teaching of the Old Testament, then this promise may not, indeed need not, have a literal fulfillment. If it can be shown, on the other hand, that the New Testament passages which refer to the new covenant in no way abrogate the new covenant with Israel or in no way assign its fulfillment to the Church, then it must be concluded that the new covenant with Israel is yet to be fulfilled if God's Word is not to be broken. If this is true, the only period in which it can be fulfilled is the millennium, and, of course, the only system of interpretation which allows for a literal millennium is premillennialism.

I. THE ISSUES INVOLVED

It is profitable always at the very outset to have in mind the issues involved. The solution of this problem concerning the new covenant with Israel hinges on three determinative issues.

First, are the promises given to Israel in the new covenant being fulfilled in this age? The answer to this question will either further justify or weaken premillennialism.

Secondly, how does the New Testament use the term *new covenant?* The answer to this question will give additional confirmation to the first and will be a basis for other conclusions.

Thirdly, what is the explicit teaching of the New Testament concerning the new covenant? The New Testament quotes from the Old Testament the major passage on the new covenant and draws certain conclusions. What these are, and their relation to the doctrine as a whole, will in large measure determine the answer to the entire question.

II. PREMILLENNIALISTS' INTERPRETATION
OF THE NEW COVENANT

Premillennialists are divided into three groups as far as their interpretation of the new covenant is concerned. This does not evince weakness, for not one of the views contradicts the system. Two views are essentially the same, and the third is the one extreme of which amillennialism is the other. This is the view that the new covenant directly concerns Israel and has no relationship to the Church. It is not denied that the Church has a covenant, but it is emphasized that this is not specifically a new covenant but rather the only covenant. This approach to the problem of interpretation is not generally held by premillennialists although J. N. Darby held this view.

The most common view among premillennialists concerning the new covenant is that which is set forth in the notes of the Scofield Reference Bible. This interpretation holds that the one new covenant has two aspects, one which applies to Israel, and one which applies to the church. These have been called the realistic and spiritual aspects of the covenant, but both aspects comprise essentially one covenant based on the sacrifice of the Lord Jesus Christ.

The third form which premillennial interpretation takes is that which distinguishes the new covenant with Israel from the new covenant with the Church. This view finds two new covenants in which the promises to Israel and the promises to the Church are more sharply distinguished even though both new covenants are based on the one sacrifice of Christ. This view does not differ essentially from the view that holds that there are two aspects to the one covenant, but it at least shows that the Scripture will support a sharp distinction between Israel and the Church which further strengthens the premillennial position. One cannot see that the one covenant, two aspects interpretation absolutely contradicts the entire premillennial system, but at least this chapter will show that another interpretation, namely two new covenants, is possible.

III. THE OLD TESTAMENT TEACHING ON THE NEW COVENANT WITH ISRAEL

The people of the new covenant. The teaching of the Old Testament is that the new covenant therein given is for the Jewish people. This is seen for several reasons.

First, it is seen by the fact of the words of establishment of the covenant. "Behold, the days come, saith the Lord, that I will make a new covenant with the house of Israel, and with the house of Judah" (Jer. 31:31). Peters points out that this verse "which as all commentators admit (however they may afterward spiritualize) in its literal aspect denotes the Jewish people." [1] Verse 33 of the same passage reaffirms the fact that the covenant is made with Israel, and this is recognized by such Old Testament scholars as Keil and Orelli even though they afterward spiritualize the truth. Other passages which support this fact are: Isaiah 59:20-21; 61:8-9; Jeremiah 32:37-40; 50:4-5; Ezekiel 16:60-63; 34:25-26; 37:21-28.

Secondly, that the Old Testament teaches that the new covenant is for Israel is also seen by the fact of its very name. In the central passage in Jeremiah 31:31-34 it is contrasted with the Mosaic covenant. Since, then, the new covenant is made with the same people as the Mosaic was, the important question is, with whom was the Mosaic covenant made? We believe that the Scripture clearly teaches that the Mosaic covenant of the law was made with the nation Israel only. Romans 2:14 defi-

[1] *Op. cit.,* I, 322.

nitely states that the law was not given to the Gentiles. Romans 6:14 and Galatians 3:24-25 show that the Christian is not under the law. Second Corinthians 3:7-11 states that the ten commandments specifically ("written and engraven in stones") are done away (verse 11). The Old Testament, to which appeal is made in this section, conclusively states that the law was for Israel only.

> These are the statutes and judgments and laws, which the Lord made between him and the children of Israel in Mount Sinai by the hand of Moses (Lev. 26:46).

> And what nation is there so great, that hath statutes and judgments so righteous as all this law, which I set before you this day? (Deut. 4:8)

There can be no question as to whom pertains the law. It is for Israel alone, and since this old covenant was made with Israel, the new covenant is made with the same people, no other group or nation being in view.

Thirdly, that the Old Testament teaches that the new covenant is for Israel is also seen by the fact that in its establishment the perpetuity of the nation Israel and her restoration to the land is vitally linked with it (Jer. 31:35-40). The Church is never called a nation, and the national aspect of this covenant concerns an earthly people. In the passage cited the points of identification, the tower of Hananeel, the hill of Gareb, and the brook Kidron, concern the city of Jerusalem. This has to be the literal city which has a geographical position in Palestine on this earth. It cannot possibly be the New Jerusalem or heavenly city, for where, for instance, in the environs of the New Jerusalem is there a "valley of the dead bodies, and of the ashes" (verse 40)? It must refer to the boundaries of the restored city of Jerusalem. *Cf.* Zechariah 14:9-11.

Thus we conclude that for these three incontrovertible reasons, the very words of the text, the name itself, and the linking with the perpetuity of the nation, the new covenant according to the teaching of the Old Testament is for the people of Israel.

The period of the new covenant. According to the teaching of the Old Testament the new covenant is yet future. Hosea regarded it as future seven hundred years before the time of Christ (2:18-20). About the same time Isaiah said, "I will make an everlasting covenant with you" (55:3). A century later Jeremiah prophesied as recorded in the thirty-first chapter already quoted. At the time of the prophecies of Ezekiel the new covenant was still future (16:60, 62;20:37; 34:25-26).

Isaiah 59:20-21 also tells the period of the new covenant, that is, when "the Redeemer shall come to Zion, and unto them that turn from transgression in Jacob." According to Romans 11:26-27, where this passage is quoted, the period of the new covenant was still future at the time of the Apostle Paul. Israel's covenant with Messiah is yet to be accomplished and that only when their iniquity has been purged by the return of Messiah.

Further, the period of the new covenant is vitally linked with the restoration of Israel to her land. Jeremiah says:

> Behold, I will gather them out of all countries, whither I have driven them in mine anger, and in my fury, and in great wrath; and I will bring them again unto this place, and I will cause them to dwell safely. . . . And I will make an everlasting covenant with them, that I will not turn away from them, to do

them good; but I will put my fear in their hearts, that they shall not depart from me. Yea, I will rejoice over them to do them good, and I will plant them in this land assuredly with my whole heart and with my whole soul (32:37, 40-41).

The sequence of events set up by the prophet is that Israel will first be regathered and restored to the land and then will experience the blessings of the new covenant *in the land*. History records no such sequence. God cannot fulfill the covenant until Israel is regathered as a nation. Her complete restoration is demanded by the new covenant, and this has not yet taken place in the history of the world. The Jewish state of Israel established in Palestine today is not the fulfillment of prophecies concerning the nation Israel in the prophetic Word. Israel is constituted as a nation in God's sight even while in dispersion, and the fact that a portion of the Jewish people have constituted themselves a political entity does not make this portion the nation of prophecy. Fulfillment of the prophecies requires the regathering of all Israel, their spiritual rebirth, and the return of Christ. Present-day Israel, though doubtless a forerunner of and a preparation for the fulfillment of the prophecies concerning Israel as a nation in the future, is characterized only by a partial return in unbelief.

Finally, it can be shown that the period of the new covenant is millennial. The following passages, which are limited to those whose contexts speak of the new covenant, give descriptions of some of the blessings to be experienced in the time of the fulfillment of the new covenant.

And they shall teach no more every man his neighbour, and every man his brother, saying, Know the Lord: for they shall

all know me, from the least of them unto the greatest of them, saith the Lord: for I will forgive their iniquity, and I will remember their sin no more (Jer. 31:34).

And I will make with them a covenant of peace, and will cause the evil beasts to cease out of the land: and they shall dwell safely in the wilderness, and sleep in the woods (Ezek. 34:25).

Both universal knowledge of the Lord and changes in the animal kingdom are millennial blessings according to Isaiah 11:6-9. Therefore, the new covenant is not only future but millennial.

For the sake of completeness a word must be added concerning the everlasting character of the covenant. The question naturally arises, does the covenant relate only to the kingdom age or is it truly everlasting? Both things are true. It begins in the millennium and is perpetuated throughout the eternal state.

The provisions of the new covenant. The following provisions for Israel, the people of the new covenant, to be fulfilled in the millennium, the period of the new covenant, are found in the Old Testament.

(1) The new covenant is an unconditional, grace covenant resting on the "I will" of God. The frequency of the use of the phrase in Jeremiah 31:31-34 is striking. *Cf.* Ezekiel 16:60-62.

(2) The new covenant is an everlasting covenant. This is closely related to the fact that it is unconditional and made in grace. The Scripture clearly says:

For I the Lord love judgment, I hate robbery for burnt-offering; and I will direct their work in truth, and I will make an everlasting covenant with them (Isa. 61:8, *cf.* Ezek. 37:26; Jer. 31:35-37).

(3) The new covenant also promises the impartation of a renewed mind and heart which we may call regeneration.

But this shall be the covenant that I will make with the house of Israel; After those days, saith the Lord, I will put my law in their inward parts, and write it in their hearts; and will be their God, and they shall be my people (Jer. 31:33, *cf.* Isa. 59:21).

(4) The new covenant provides for restoration to the favor and blessing of God.

And I will betroth thee unto me for ever; yea, I will betroth thee unto me in righteousness, and in judgment, and in lovingkindness, and in mercies. I will even betroth thee unto me in faithfulness: and thou shalt know the Lord (Hos. 2:19-20, *cf* Isa. 61:9).

(5) Forgiveness of sin is also included in the covenant, "for I will remove their iniquity, and I will remember their sin no more" (Jer. 31:34b).

(6) The indwelling of the Holy Spirit is also included. This is seen by comparing Jeremiah 31:33 with Ezekiel 36:27.

(7) The teaching ministry of the Holy Spirit will be manifested, and the will of God will be known by obedient hearts.

And they shall teach no more every man his neighbour, and every man his brother, saying, Know the Lord: for they shall all know me, from the least of them unto the greatest of them, saith the Lord (Jer. 31:34).

(8) As is always the case when Israel is in the land, she will be blessed materially in accordance with the provisions of the new covenant. Jeremiah declares that God "will rejoice over them to do them good" (32:41), and Isaiah says that He "will direct their work in truth" (61:8). As a part of this blessing the land will again be their own, for God has promised that He "will plant them in this land assuredly with . . . [His] whole heart and . . . soul" (Jer. 32:41). Beasts will be tamed and nature will again function according to the best interests of the productivity of the soil (Ezek. 34:25-27).

(9) The sanctuary will be rebuilt in Jerusalem, for it is written "I . . . will set my sanctuary in the midst of them for evermore. My tabernacle also shall be with them" (Ezek. 37:26-27a).

(10) War shall cease and peace shall reign according to Hosea 2:18. The fact that this is also a definite characteristic of the millennium (Isa. 2:4) further supports the fact that the new covenant is millennial in its fulfillment.

(11) The blood of the Lord Jesus Christ is the foundation of all the blessings of the new covenant, for "by the blood of thy covenant I have sent forth thy prisoners out of the pit wherein is no water" (Zech. 9:11).

By way of summary, it may be said that as far as the Old Testament teaching on the new covenant is concerned, the covenant was made with the Jewish people. Its period of fulfillment is yet future beginning when the Deliverer shall come and continuing throughout all eternity. Its provisions for the nation Israel are glorious, and they all rest and depend on the very Word of God.

IV. THE NEW TESTAMENT TEACHING ON THE NEW COVENANT WITH ISRAEL

This is the most crucial section in the consideration of the new covenant. The important factors to be considered are the use of the term *new covenant* and the actual teaching of the New Testament on the new covenant. The premillennial system has been justified by the Old Testament teaching concerning the new covenant, for the provisions have not been fulfilled in this present age. Now the question is, does the New Testament change all this? If it does, premillennialism is weakened; if not, it is further strengthened, all of which shows the vital relationship that exists between the new covenant and the premillennial system.

The use of the term in the New Testament. The term *new covenant* is used in five undisputed New Testament passages:

Likewise also the cup after supper, saying, This cup is the new testament in my blood, which is shed for you (Luke 22:20).

After the same manner also he took the cup, when he had supped, saying, This cup is the new testament in my blood: this do ye, as oft as ye drink it, in remembrance of me (1 Cor. 11:25).

Who also hath made us able ministers of the new testament; not of the letter, but of the spirit: for the letter killeth, but the spirit giveth life (2 Cor. 3:6).

For finding fault with them, he saith, Behold, the days come, saith the Lord, when I will make a new covenant with the house of Israel and with the house of Judah (Heb. 8:8).

And for this cause he is the mediator of the new testament, that by means of death, for the redemption of the transgressions that were under the first testament, they which are called might receive the promise of eternal inheritance (Heb. 9:15).

In addition, there are six further references to the new covenant in the New Testament.

For this is the blood of the new testament, which is shed for many for the remission of sins (Matt. 26:28).

And he said unto them, This is my blood of the new testament, which is shed for many (Mk. 14:24).

For this is my covenant unto them, when I shall take away their sins (Rom. 11:27).

For this is the covenant that I will make with the house of Israel after those days, saith the Lord; I will put my laws into their mind, and write them in their hearts: and I will be to them a God, and they shall be to me a people (Heb. 8:10).

In that he saith, A new covenant, he hath made the first old. Now that which decayeth and waxeth old is ready to vanish away (Heb. 10:13).

And to Jesus the mediator of the new covenant, and to the blood of sprinkling, that speaketh better things than that of Abel (Heb. 12:24).

The word *new* is not mentioned in Matthew 26:28; Mark 14:24; Romans 11:27; and Hebrews 8:10, although it is found in some texts of the Gospel references. A critical study of the text is not necessary, for it is clear from the parallel references in Luke 22:20 and First Corinthians 11:25 that the references in Matthew and Mark also refer to the new covenant. The contexts of Romans 11:27 and Hebrews 8:10 clearly indicate that the new covenant is in view in these passages even though the word *new* is not used. In Hebrews 12:24 the word νέα is used instead of the usual adjective καινή, which brings out the fact that the covenant is recent in its beginning as well as new in quality.

The use of the term in the first two references, Luke 22:20 and First Corinthians 11:25, is in connection with the Lord's Supper. Since the Lord's Supper is an ordinance of the Christian Church and is for both Jew and Gentile, it is obvious that the new covenant as referred to in the New Testament is not entirely Jewish. In fact, there must be a new covenant according to the teaching of the New Testament that is made with the Church. It is of this same covenant that Paul was a minister (2 Cor. 3:6), and since he was a minister to the Gentiles, the scope of this new covenant must be different from the one revealed in the Old Testament.

Hebrews 9:15 teaches that the Lord Jesus Christ is the mediator of the new covenant. The death of Christ is necessary to the assuring of the provisions of the new covenant which He makes in His death. This may seem like arguing in a circle, but this is exactly what the writer states. In this same Epistle is the final reference to the new covenant (8:8), and this is the only New Testament reference which clearly relates the term *new covenant* to Israel. This is the determining reference in relation to the premillennial system; it will be studied in detail.

Before doing that, however, we must emphasize that the new covenant as instituted at the Lord's Supper was extended to include other than the Jewish people, for it was "for many" (Matt. 26:28; Mk. 14:24). One cannot deny that the Church receives similar blessings to those of the new covenant with

Israel, but *similarity is not fulfillment*. Regeneration, indwelling of the Holy Spirit, teaching of the Holy Spirit, and forgiveness of sins, which are the four important blessings promised to Israel in Jeremiah 31:31-34, are all promised to those who believe on Christ in this age. In the light of these facts, could it not be that there is a new covenant for the Church as well as a new covenant for Israel?

If the Church does not have a new covenant then she is fulfilling Israel's promises, for it has been shown that the Old Testament teaches that the new covenant is for Israel alone. If the Church is fulfilling Israel's promises as contained in the new covenant or anywhere in Scripture, then premillennialism is weakened. One might well ask why there are not two aspects to one new covenant. This may be the case, and it is the position held by many premillennialists, but we agree that the amillennialist has every right to say of this view that it is "a practical admission that the new covenant is fulfilled in and to the Church." [2] However, since the New Testament will support two new covenants, is it not more consistent premillennialism to consider that Israel and the Church each has a new covenant?

What, then, is the old covenant with the Church? Some premillennialists would answer that the so-called Adamic covenant (Gen. 3:14-19) is to the new covenant with the Church as the Mosaic covenant is to the new covenant with Israel. This may be so, but why is there any need for an old covenant with the Church if the word *new* means new in quality? A new quality does not demand at all a contrasting old quality. In either case, this does not affect the premillennial system of interpretation.

[2] Allis, *op. cit.*, p. 155.

We have demonstrated that there is a possible solution which is consistent with the system, and that is sufficient.

The use of the Old Testament quotations of the new covenant in the New Testament. It is now necessary to consider what use the New Testament makes of the quotations of the new covenant from the Old Testament. This section will strengthen the conclusion of the previous section that there are two new covenants by showing that the New Testament teaches that the new covenant with Israel is yet future and that the promises are in no way abrogated or assigned to the Church. The principal passage to be considered is Hebrews 8:6-13 with references to Hebrews 10:16-17 and Romans 11:26-27. In order to discover the teaching of these passages, five questions must be answered.

First, who are the people addressed? The Epistle to the Hebrews is, as its title indicates, addressed to Jewish people. It was written to Hebrew converts and treats Hebrew institutions. The point is simply this: in an Epistle addressed to Jewish believers one would expect to find a reference to Israel's covenants and in particular to the new covenant with Israel. Admittedly, the fact that this is an Epistle to Hebrews certainly does not prove that the new covenant therein mentioned is the one with Israel, but it is supporting evidence to this fact.

Secondly, what is the proof intended? The plan of the Epistle is to show the contrast between Judaism and the better things of Christianity. The writer has shown in the earlier chapters that Christ is better than angels, than Moses, than Joshua, and than Aaron. In chapter 8 he continues by showing that Christianity has a better covenant than Judaism and Christ is the mediator of this better covenant established on better promises (8:6). The writer proves this by contrasting the Mosaic covenant. This covenant was never eternal, and this is proved to these people of Jewish background by quoting from the Old Testament the central passage on the new covenant. This shows that even the Old Testament anticipated the temporary character of the Mosaic covenant; nevertheless, Christians by contrast have a better covenant.

Thirdly, what is the purpose of the quotation? As intimated above, the purpose of the quotation from Jeremiah 31 is to show from the Old Testament Scriptures that the Mosaic covenant is not eternal. Amillennial exegesis attempts to make this passage prove that the church is now fulfilling Israel's promises. Allis says:

> The passage speaks of the new covenant. It declares that this new covenant has been already introduced and that by virtue of the fact it is called "new" it has made the one which it is replacing "old," and that the old is about to vanish away. It would be hard to find a clearer reference to the gospel age in the Old Testament than in these verses in Jeremiah.[3]

Walvoord has well answered this by saying:

> Dr. Allis has stated well the amillennial position, and has also himself indicated its fallacy, in the opinion of the writer, by begging the question. He states that the Hebrews passage "declares that this new covenant has been already introduced." The passage states that a "better covenant" than the Mosaic covenant has been introduced (Heb. 8:6), but it does not state here or anywhere else that this better covenant is identical with the "new covenant with the house of Israel," or that the new covenant with Israel has been introduced. The argument of the passage does not hinge on this point at all, but rather on

[3] *Op. cit.,* p. 154.

whether the Old Testament in any way anticipated an end to the Mosaic covenant. This the Old Testament does, but it does not follow that the new covenant of the Old Testament is identical with the better covenant of Hebrews.[4]

Indeed it would follow that the better covenant of Hebrews is that which the Lord Jesus established with the Church, that is, the new covenant with the Church. This means that the writer of the Epistle has referred to both new covenants, and by his reference to the new covenant with Israel in the quotation from Jeremiah 31, he shows that it has not been annulled. It is important to notice that nowhere does the writer say that the covenant with Israel is fulfilled. Indeed that is the reason for the lack of appeal to the content of the covenant. As Walvoord further says:

> There is no appeal at all to the content of the new covenant with Israel as being identical with the better covenant of which Hebrews speaks. The very absence of such an appeal is as strong as any argument from silence can be. It would have been a crushing blow to the opponents of the Christian order among the Jews to be faced with a quotation which described in detail the promises of God to the church. The writer instead merely refers to the word *new* and goes on to show in Hebrews nine how the Christian order superseded the sacraments of the Mosaic covenant.[5]

In Hebrews 10:16-17 there is another quotation of the new covenant with Israel, and the problem of interpretation is much the same. The argument here is that the sacrifice of Christ supersedes the sacrifices under the Mosaic covenant, and the appeal to the new covenant with Israel is to show that the

[4] *Bibliotheca Sacra,* CIII, 18-19.
[5] *Ibid.,* p. 25.

Old Testament Scriptures promised that sins would be remembered no more. The passage does not state that the new covenant with Israel is identical with the new covenant with the Church or that it is fulfilled by the Church.

Fourthly, what people are concerned? It quite naturally follows from a right understanding of the Jeremiah quotation in Hebrews 8 that the people in view are the Jewish people. In other words, the New Testament does not disannul the promises of God to Israel as contained in the new covenant with Israel. Furthermore, the New Testament verifies the Old Testament teaching that the people of the new covenant are Israel. Amillennial exegesis makes "the house of Israel and the house of Judah" mean the people of God in general. On what basis such statements are made is beyond imagination. One would like to ask how the Old Testament Scriptures are to be handled, especially the curses on Israel, if passages specifically addressed to the Jews are for all men also. This is certainly not sound exegesis of the words *Israel* and *Judah*. The new covenant of Hebrews 8:7-13 belongs to the Jewish people and not to the Church.

Fifthly, what is the period of fulfillment? Although Hebrews 8 does not make any explicit statement concerning the time of fulfillment of the new covenant with Israel, the passage does imply that it is still unfulfilled. It has been seen that there is no appeal to the content of the new covenant as would have been the case if the writer were saying that it is now fulfilled. However, there is in the New Testament one additional quotation of the central Old Testament passage on the new covenant which clearly states the time of fulfillment of the yet unfulfilled new covenant with Israel. The passage is Romans 11:26-27:

> And so all Israel shall be saved: as it is written, There shall come out of Sion the Deliverer, and shall turn away ungodliness from Jacob: For this is my covenant unto them, when I shall take away their sins.

Verse 27 is obviously a reference to the new covenant with Israel (*cf.* Jer. 31:34); therefore, a right understanding of the period of fulfillment of this passage will tell us the period of fulfillment of the new covenant with Israel. At this point amillennialists are divided. Some hold that "all Israel" means all believers. Evidently Allis is among this group although he passes by Romans 11:26 with only a footnote reference in which he tries to show that Romans 11 says nothing of Israel's restoration. He argues that Paul is not speaking of Israel's restoration because he does not speak of restoration to the land, which is certainly no argument at all. However, this view of the meaning of "all Israel" is consistent amillennialism, for if the new covenant is now assigned to believers then "all Israel" must also refer to all believers.

Many amillennialists, on the other hand, admit on the basis of careful exegesis that Israel must mean Israel. Usually they say that "all Israel" refers to the elect remnant of Israel. Although they interpret the passage literally, they will not admit a group deliverance of the nation Israel but only an individual deliverance. Here their dilemma shows the inconsistency of the amillennial position, for if all Israel is to be saved on the basis of the new covenant, as Romans 11:25-26 states,

and if "all Israel" means the remnant of the Jews, then the
new covenant is still with the Jews and not with the Church,
even though, according to amillennialism, it is being fulfilled
in this present age!

The premillennial position and teaching of the passage is
that Israel will be restored as a nation at the Second Coming
of Christ. In Romans 11 Paul has been considering the setting
aside of Israel as a nation, and likewise the restoration is as a
nation. This will take place when the Deliverer comes out of
Zion, that is, at Christ's Second Coming, and *at this same time*
God will fulfill the promises to Israel contained in the new
covenant. Thus the New Testament instead of assigning the
new covenant a present fulfillment in the Church, teaches not
only that it is as yet unfulfilled but also that it will be fulfilled
to Israel at the Second Coming of Christ.

V. CONCLUSION

In considering, first of all, the teaching of the Old Testament we have concluded that the new covenant is for Israel,
and if language means anything at all, this means the natural
descendants of Abraham through Jacob. Also the Old Testament teaches that the new covenant is yet future, and by
comparing millennial passages it is clear that the period of
fulfillment is the millennium.

The occurrences of the term *new covenant* in the New Testament show that there is a wider meaning than to Israel alone.
Some of the blessings of the new covenant with Israel are blessings which we enjoy now as members of the body of Christ,
and on this basis it was concluded that there is a new cove-

nant with the Church. This is substantiated by the teaching of the New Testament, for the Scripture nowhere abrogates the new covenant with Israel or assigns its fulfillment to the Church. Indeed, the New Testament explicitly states that the new covenant with Israel will be fulfilled at the Second Coming of Christ. Hebrews 8 quotes the new covenant with *Israel* only to show that the Old Testament anticipated an end to the Mosaic covenant and that Christians have a better covenant, that is, the new covenant with the Church.

In all of this, premillennialism has been confirmed. Israel means Israel and her promises have not been fulfilled by the Church. Since they have not, they must be fulfilled in the millennium if God's Word is not to be broken. The induction that there are two new covenants strengthens the premillennial position and does not permit the amillennialist to say that the Church is fulfilling Israel's promises. Thus, again, premillennialism rests on a firm basis in the teaching of the Word of God concerning the new covenant.

Chapter 7

Its Basis in
ECCLESIOLOGY

In ecclesiology, the doctrine of the Church, premillennialism has a firm basis. It was stated in the introduction that premillennial interpretation extends to the whole system of doctrine, and while it is impossible here to state the entire premillennial doctrine of ecclesiology it is necessary to relate certain features of ecclesiology in which premillennialism has its roots.

The main point in question is whether or not the Church is a distinct body in this present age. If the Church is not a subject of Old Testament prophecy, then the Church is not fulfilling Israel's promises, but instead Israel herself must fulfill them and that in the future. In brief, premillennialism with a dispensational view recognizes the Church as a distinct entity, distinct from Israel in her beginning, in her relation to this age, and in her promises. If the Church is not a distinct body, then the door is open wide for amillennialism to enter with its ideas that the Church is some sort of full-bloomed development of Judaism and the fulfiller of Israel's promises of blessing (but not of judgment). Thus premillennialism and ecclesiology are inseparably related.

Since the entire field of ecclesiology cannot be covered, the argument will be along these lines. First of all it is necessary to see if the Scriptures, in setting forth the program of God for Israel, allow for an interposition of this church age. Then it must be proved whether or not the designation of the Church as a mystery means that it was unknown to the Old Testament prophets. Finally one must examine the teaching of the Scripture concerning the use of the word *church* to see if the Church is a distinct body in this age.

I. THE CHURCH, AN INTERCALATION

The first question asked above is answered by the teaching of the Scriptures that the Church is an intercalation. It makes little difference to the doctrine whether one wishes to call the Church a parenthesis or an intercalation, but since a parenthesis is related primarily to grammar and an intercalation does mean an introduction of a period of time into a calendar, the latter word seems more accurate. Allis admits that "the parenthesis view of the Church is the inevitable result of the doctrine that Old Testament prophecy must be fulfilled literally to Israel," [1] and yet he endeavors to prove that there is no idea of a parenthesis in Scripture.

No originality is claimed here, and since H. A. Ironside has done an exhaustive piece of work, his conclusions will merely be summarized.[2] These illustrations show that there is abundant Scripture evidence for a parenthesis or intercalation. This being true, then it will have been demonstrated that in the Scripture's setting forth of God's program for Israel there is allowance made for the interpolation of this present church age.

[1] *Op. cit.*, p. 54.
[2] *The Great Parenthesis*, pp. 15-131.

Daniel 9:24-27. While the explanation of all the details of this prophecy is not within the scope of this chapter, certain facts are important to the discussion. The prophecy concerns the nation Israel, for the angel speaks of Daniel's people (verse 24). The prophecy concerns seventy weeks of years which are divided into seven weeks (49 years), sixty-two weeks (434 years) and one week (7 years). The beginning of the reckoning is the twentieth year of Artaxerxes, 445 B.C. According to Sir Robert Anderson's calculations, the Lord Jesus Christ entered Jerusalem exactly sixty-nine weeks of years later. Therefore there remains but one week to be fulfilled, and since the first sixty-nine have been fulfilled literally, it may be expected that the seventieth will be fulfilled in the same manner. Clearly there is an interval of time between the sixty-ninth and seventieth weeks, and the interval is the church age.

Isaiah 61:2-3. When the Lord Jesus Christ was reading in the synagogue at Nazareth (Luke 4:16-19) He read from this passage in Isaiah, but He significantly stopped the reading with the words "the acceptable year of the Lord" even though the Isaiah passage goes on to speak of "the day of vengeance of our God." The Lord, however, was distinguishing between the events connected with His first coming and those of His Second Coming. He did not continue the reading because He knew that the events of Isaiah 61 were not continuous and that the day of vengeance of our God was not due to begin at that time. In other words, the Lord Jesus made room for the parenthesis of this church age which has already lasted more than nineteen hundred years.

Daniel 2. In this chapter which sets forth the times of the Gentiles, the parenthesis occurs within the Roman empire. The last condition of the empire, symbolized by the feet with the ten toes, has never existed, for there have never arisen these ten kingdoms *at the same time*. This same parenthesis is seen between verses 23 and 24 of the seventh chapter, between 8:22 and 23, and between 11:35 and 36. These passages should be studied in detail, but the only point to be made here is that the Old Testament allows for the present age although it does not foresee it.

In Hosea. In Hosea 3:4-5 the gap occurs again, for the "afterward" indicates the long period of time during which Israel is wandering among the nations. Again, in the last verse of chapter 5, there is reference to the ascension of the Lord and in the first verses of chapter 6 to Israel's repentance. The ascension took place nearly two thousand years ago, but the events of chapter 6 have not yet taken place.

In the Psalms. Ironside lists three Psalms which give examples of the intercalation period. In Psalm 22:1-21 the sufferings of the Lord on the cross are pictured. Verse 22 tells of His Resurrection and appearance among His own, but verse 23 sets forth the coming of the kingdom and deliverance of Israel. Surely this is yet future for it is not true that "all the ends of the world . . . remember and turn unto the Lord" (verse 27). Psalm 110:1 speaks of the present work of Christ —"sit thou at my right hand"—and the second verse of His return in power. Again it is evident that this is unfulfilled for surely today He does not "rule . . . in the midst of thine enemies." Psalm 34:12-16 affords another illustration of this parenthesis principle because it is partially quoted by Peter (1 Pet. 3:10-12).

Israel's ecclesiastical year. Leviticus 23 also gives a further picture of the parenthesis. In the spring of the year occurred the feasts of Passover, firstfruits, and Pentecost, all of which have already had a fulfillment in the death of Christ, in the Resurrection of Christ, and in the descent of the Holy Spirit. In the fall of the year, beginning with the seventh month, occurred three more feasts, trumpets, atonement, and tabernacles. Trumpets have to do with the calling back of Israel to her land (Isa. 18:3-7; 27:12-13); atonement, with Israel's cleansing (Zech. 12:10-14; 13:1); and tabernacles, with Israel's millennial blessings. The break between the two sets of feasts is clear and definite, and illustrative of this principle.

Romans 11. The figure of the olive tree has already been discussed under the Abrahamic covenant but is further illustration of this truth.

Acts 15. This chapter concerning the first church council at Jerusalem has also been discussed and is merely listed here to give added support to the argument.

These then are the evidences that show that Scripture clearly gives a place for the present church age. God's program for Israel allows room for the present age without nullifying that part of Israel's program which is yet future. The Old Testament prophets saw everything in one continuous view because the revelation of the Church in this age had not been given to them. Nevertheless place has been left for the intercalation period. The Church is an intercalation.

II. THE CHURCH, A MYSTERY

The second step in the argument is to show that the Church, though allowed for in the prophecies of old, was not foreseen in the Old Testament; that is, that it is a mystery not revealed until New Testament times.

Definition of a mystery. The word *mystery* does not necessarily mean something difficult to be understood but something that is imparted only to the initiated, something that is unknown until it is revealed. In the English Old Testament the word never appears, and μυστήριον is used in the Septuagint only in Daniel 2:18, 19, 27-30, 47 as a translation of the word *secret* in reference to the king's dream. In the New Testament the word is used twenty-seven times of which twenty occurrences are in the Pauline Epistles. It is somewhat significant that the word is not used in the Old Testament. It would point to the fact that a mystery is a New Testament truth. It is also significant that Paul is the one who uses the word the most, and as a result we may conclude that Romans 16:25 defines a mystery.

Does the Scripture support this definition that a mystery is a truth hidden in the Old Testament but now revealed in the New Testament? The chief point of difference with the amillennialist concerns whether or not the truth of a mystery was *completely* hidden in the Old Testament. Allis stresses this, using as his proof Ephesians 3:5, "Which in other ages was not made known unto the sons of men, as it is now revealed unto his holy apostles and prophets by the Spirit," and emphasizes the word *as*. In answer to this, Payne points out:

Had he given more attention to the similar passage in Colossians 1:26 it might have altered the direction of his argument. This passage, which Allis simply indicates with a Scripture reference, makes it quite clear that Paul did not intend the *as* in Ephesians 3:5 to introduce a qualifying phrase; for in Colossians it is replaced with a *but* which eliminates the possibility of the qualifying interpretation.[3]

Since this chief argument which the amillennialist advances does not stand up, then it may be assumed that the definition that a mystery is a truth completely hidden in the Old Testament but revealed in the New Testament is valid. This will be true throughout the entire New Testament if the specific item which is designated as a mystery is kept in view.

Is the Church a mystery? It is true that the Church itself is never actually called a mystery in the New Testament. However, it is a mystery since its major elements are specifically designated as mysteries.

The mystery of the one body is revealed in Ephesians 3:1-12. In a word, it is that the Gentiles would be fellowheirs with the Jews, a thing absolutely foreign to the Jewish mind. In Ephesians 2:15, Paul calls the body a "new man." This is a difficult phrase for the amillennialist because it is the Word of God, not Darby, which says that the Church is a new man and not a made-over Israel.

The mystery of the organism, referred to in Colossians 1:24-27; 2:10-19; 3:4, 11, is that Christ indwells each believer. Israel was never spoken of as a living organism of all Jews, and only Christ's external manifestation was anticipated by the Old Testament. That is the reason that "Christ in you" is a mystery.

There is the mystery of the bride. Although the Church is not actually called the bride, the symbolism used in Ephesians 5:22-32 of the husband and wife relationship and the marriage

---

[3] *Amillennial Theology As a System*, pp. 197-98.

recorded in Revelation 19:7-9 indicate that the Church is the bride of Christ. There is no mystery of the bridegroom relationship to Israel (Isa. 54:5), but such a relationship with the Church was not revealed until New Testament times.

Finally there is the mystery of the rapture. The idea of resurrection was not unknown to Old Testament saints, but the idea of the translation of living saints at the rapture was the mystery revealed through Paul in First Corinthians 15:51-52. This passage cannot refer to the Second Coming of Christ because that event was not a mystery unrevealed in the Old Testament. The reference is to something distinct, that is, the rapture of the Church before the tribulation.

If the argument was correct that the church age comes between the sixty-ninth and seventieth weeks of Daniel, and if this passage reveals how the Church will be taken out of the world before the seventieth week begins, then the end of the church age is before the tribulation. This also follows from the character of the Church as a mystery.

A related passage is First Thessalonians 4:13-18 in which Paul speaks of the same event (because he talks of the translation of the living) and he speaks of it as a comforting hope. Of what comfort would the hope of the rapture be if the church is to pass through the tribulation if that time is as terrible as it is described to be? The Thessalonians had evidently been concerned about the relationship of those who had died to the kingdom. Paul reassures them by saying that those who have died God will bring *with* Jesus (verse 14). The reason that God can bring these believers with Him at His Second Coming into the kingdom is because *before* that time God will have raised them, and Paul then goes on to speak of that resurrection and translation which must occur before His Second Coming.

The conclusion is easily reached. Since the fundamental characteristics of the Church are called mysteries, the Church itself is a mystery, that is, it was not foreseen in the Old Testament but revealed only in the New Testament.

The termini of the church. To support the argument that the Church is a distinct work of God in this age, this brief section concerning the termini of the Church is apropos. It has just been shown that the Church is limited to the New Testament. Chafer has given four incontrovertible reasons why the Church began at the day of Pentecost.[4] (1) The Church could not have existed in the world until after the death of Christ, for her purification is solely by His precious blood and she is built on His finished work. (2) The Church could not have existed until after the Resurrection of Christ, for He, the risen One, is the one who provides her with resurrection life. (3) There could be no Church until Christ had ascended into heaven, for she is the body of which He is the head, and this relationship was established by His ascension. Neither could the Church survive for a moment without His intercessory work. (4) Finally, the Church could not come into being before Pentecost because the advent of the Holy Spirit did not occur until then. If the Church is the body of Christ (Eph. 1:22-23), if entrance to the body of Christ is through the baptism of the Holy Spirit (1 Cor. 12:13), and if the baptism of the Holy Spirit did not occur until the day of Pentecost (Acts 1:5; 2:4; 11:15-16), then the Church did not begin until the day of Pentecost.

4 *Systematic Theology*, IV, 45-46.

By the same argument, that is, the relation of the Holy Spirit to the Church, there is the indication of the end of the church age. Without entering into all the arguments concerning whether or not the Church will go through the tribulation, let it simply be noticed that, since according to 2 Thessalonians 2:1-12 the lawless one who is an important personage connected with the beginning of the tribulation cannot be revealed until the Holy Spirit is removed, the Church, the bodies of whose members are the temples of the Holy Spirit, must also be removed before the tribulation period begins. Thiessen gives the correct view of this passage when he says:

> . . . that which "withholdeth" (neuter, verse 6) and "he who letteth" (hindereth) (masculine, verse 7), is none other than the Holy Spirit. He, no doubt, employs human government and human laws, as also providential interventions, in the accomplishment of His purposes, . . . but more especially the testimony and influence of the Church. . . . When the Church is caught up, the Holy Spirit will be taken from the world in the peculiar sense in which He is present on earth today. . . . He will no longer be here in the same degree of manifestation. He will be here at that time in some such way as He was present in the world before the Day of Pentecost.[5]

The termini of the Church, from Pentecost to the rapture, support the fact that the Church is a mystery, which fact in turn supports the premillennial system of interpretation.

III. THE CHURCH, A DISTINCT BODY OF SAINTS IN THIS AGE

The last proposition in the argument of this chapter is to consider whether or not the Church is a distinct body of saints

[5] *Will the Church Pass Through the Tribulation?* p. 41.

in this age. That this is true is practically a self-evident conclusion from the arguments already stated. These facts have already been pointed out:

(1) The Church is not fulfilling in any sense the promises to Israel.

(2) The use of the word *Church* in the New Testament never includes unsaved Israelites.

(3) The church age is not seen in God's program for Israel. It is an intercalation.

(4) The Church is a mystery in the sense that it was completely unrevealed in the Old Testament and now revealed in the New Testament.

(5) The Church did not begin until the day of Pentecost and will be removed from this world at the rapture which precedes the Second Coming of Christ.

To these reasons we now add two additional ones to show that the Church is a distinct body of saints in this age.

(6) The first use of the word *Church* in the New Testament indicates that it is still future. The word is first used in Matthew 16:18, and this first use, as with most Biblical terms, is of most important signification. In this verse these words of the Lord Jesus are recorded: "And I say also unto thee, That thou art Peter, and upon this rock I will build my church; and the gates of hell shall not prevail against it." The important word for the present discussion is the word *will*. Chafer has well pointed out that:

When the stress falls on the word *will*, the prophetic aspect is introduced and the reader is reminded that the Church did not exist at the moment Christ was speaking, but was to be realized in the future. This is a difficult aspect of truth for those who contend that the Church has existed throughout the period covered by the Old Testament, or any part of it.[6]

Thus, at the time of Christ's earthly ministry the Church was yet future.

(7) The use of the word ἐκκλησία supports the conclusion that the Church is a distinct body of saints in this age. It is used to mean simply an assembly. This is the common use of the word in the Septuagint. It is used to translate מוֹעֵד, עֵדָה, and קָהָל, all of which are translated by these words: assembly, feast, congregation, company, appointed meeting. The point is that in every case the thought is that of an assembly. In the New Testament the word is also used in this sense in Acts 7:38; 19:39; and Hebrews 2:12. This sense has no theological meaning.

It is used to mean an assembly of Christians. In this sense it may mean a local group of believers (1 Cor. 1:2; 1 Thess. 1:1; etc.) or it may mean a number of local groups (Acts 8:1, 3; 11:22; etc.).

The word is also used of the totality of professing Christians without reference to locality. Examples of this use are Acts 12:1; Romans 16:16; Galatians 1:13; etc.

It is used of the body of Christ. In this sense the word has reference to those who have been baptised into the body of Christ by the Holy Spirit (1 Cor. 12:13). This is the technical use of the word.

All agree that ἐκκλησία as used in the first-named instance is used of Israel in the Old Testament. The question is, is it used of Israel in the other senses? The answer is *no* for two

[6] *Op. cit.,* IV, 41.

reasons. All the references to Israel in the Old and New Testaments can be classified under the first use of the word; that is, in its simple meaning of an assembly; and it is not possible to use the meaning *assembly* in the technical sense which refers to the body of Christ. Of course an Israelite who accepts Christ is translated from the Old Testament assembly and put into the body of Christ, but natural Israel remains natural Israel, and the Church in the technical sense is strictly limited to those who have accepted Christ in this age. Therefore, the Church is a distinct body of saints in this age.

The original question of this chapter has been answered. The Church is a distinct body in this age. This has been shown in that the Church is an intercalation allowed for in Old Testament prophecies, in that it is a mystery revealed only in the New Testament, and in the positive proofs that the Church is a distinct body of saints in this age. Since this is so, the Church is not fulfilling Israel's promises, but she will be taken out of the way before God again deals with Israel. The only system of interpretation that allows for this distinct body, the Church, is premillennialism. Other systems cannot offer a clear-cut ecclesiology because they do not see this distinct divine purpose for this age. Israel has to be carried over into the Church, for there is no future age in other systems in which the promises to Israel can be fulfilled. Premillennialism, then, is vitally related to ecclesiology and supported firmly by it.

Chapter 8

Its Basis in
ESCHATOLOGY

Although other parts of the book have dealt with eschatological details, there are certain passages which have not been discussed which belong to the field of eschatology. In this chapter these will be considered in the relationship of premillennialism to the tribulation and to the millennium. Also some of the problems of the premillennial system will be included. One thing, however, should be very evident; that is, the proportionate place given to eschatology *per se* as a basis of the premillennial faith. Premillennialism is far more than a system of interpretation of the doctrine of last things. It is vitally related to the entire Word of God.

I. THE TRIBULATION

Premillennialism does not stand or fall on one's view of the tribulation. It is not the decisive issue, but it is hoped that the view set forth in this chapter will add to the weight of evidence that premillennialism is the only consistent system of interpretation.

The duration of the tribulation. According to Daniel 9:24-27, the period of the tribulation is seven years. Matthew 24:22

seems to indicate that this seven year period will be shortened
a little, but, generally speaking, the duration of the tribulation
is seven years. It was demonstrated that the first sixty-nine
weeks of Daniel's prophecy ended at the death of Christ and
that the seventieth week is still future. This is important because it proves that the tribulation is still future. Daniel 9:27
confirms this:

> And he shall confirm the covenant with many for one week:
> and in the midst of the week he shall cause the sacrifice and the
> oblation to cease, and for the overspreading of abominations he
> shall make it desolate, even until the consummation, and that
> determined shall be poured upon the desolate.

The important question in the interpretation involves the
antecedent of the pronoun *he*. The reference cannot be to Christ
for He did none of the things referred to in the verse. Thiessen
sets forth the correct interpretation when he says:

> It is more natural to refer the pronoun "he" to the prince
> mentioned in the last part of verse 26, namely the Roman
> prince; however not to Vespasian, Roman emperor from A.D.
> 69-79, nor to his son and successor, Titus, who ruled from A.D.
> 79-81. Neither of these made and broke a covenant with the
> Jews; and Titus lived only two years after his accession to the
> throne. The reference is to a Roman prince who shall come after
> the long interval of the last half of verse 26, which has already
> lasted 1,900 years; and the last week is still future.[1]

Daniel also indicates in this verse that the tribulation is
divided into two equal parts. The latter half is called the great
tribulation and is referred to elsewhere in Scripture as time,

[1] *Bibliotheca Sacra*, XCII, 49.

times, and half a time; that is, three and a half years (*cf*. Dan. 7:25; 12:7; Rev. 12:14). Elsewhere it is called forty-two months and 1,260 days (Rev. 11:2; 13:5; 11:3; 12:6). Thus the tribulation is a future period of approximately seven years divided into two equal parts. The fact that this period is yet future will be even more evident as the characteristics of the period are given.

The nature of the tribulation. The Scripture gives certain characteristics of this period.

First, it is a unique period.

> Alas! for that day is great, so that none is like it: it is even the time of Jacob's trouble; but he shall be saved out of it (Jer. 30:7).

> And at that time shall Michael stand up, the great prince which standeth for the children of thy people: and there shall be a time of trouble, such as never was since there was a nation even to that same time: and at that time thy people shall be delivered, every one that shall be found written in the book (Dan. 12:1).

> For then shall be great tribulation, such as was not since the beginning of the world to this time, no, nor ever shall be (Matt. 24:21).

Secondly, it is a period of judgment upon the nations. It would not be practical to enter into all the arguments concerning the interpretation of the Revelation. In contrast to the futurist interpretation assumed here, suffice it to say that:

> The most fanciful effort of imagination is demanded when the world-transforming judgments of Revelation, chapters 6-19, are applied to past history. A few writers have attempted this

adjustment in detail. More of them prefer to remain in the realm of indefinite generalities, and to excuse their own uncertainty by the contention that the Revelation is veiled and obscure at best.[2]

The entire fourteen chapters could be cited in proof of this characteristic, but a few verses are sufficient:

> And the kings of the earth, and the great men, and the rich men, and the chief captains, and the mighty men, and every bondman, and every free man, hid themselves in the rocks of the mountains; And said to the mountains and rocks, Fall on us, and hide us from the face of him that sitteth on the throne, and from the wrath of the Lamb (Rev. 6:15-16).

> And the nations were angry, and thy wrath is come, and the time of the dead, that they should be judged and that thou . . . shouldest destroy them which destroy the earth (Rev. 11:18).

Thirdly, it will be a period of persecution of Israel.

> Then shall they deliver you up to be afflicted, and shall kill you: and ye shall be hated of all nations for my name's sake. . . . And except those days should be shortened, there should no flesh be saved (Matt. 24:9, 22a).

> And the dragon was wroth with the woman, and went to make war with the remnant of her seed, which keep the commandments of God, and have the testimony of Jesus Christ (Rev. 12:17).

Fourthly, it will be a period of salvation. It is usually charged that premillennialism teaches that all who enter the tribulation period are irrevocably lost. This is not true, for the Scripture says:

[2] Chafer, *op. cit.*, IV, 361.

> And I heard the number of them which were sealed: and there were sealed an hundred and forty and four thousand of all the tribes of the children of Israel (Rev. 7:4).

> After this I beheld, and, lo, a great multitude, which no man could number, of all nations, and kindreds, and people, and tongues, stood before the throne, and before the Lamb, clothed with white robes, and palms in their hands; And cried with a loud voice, saying, Salvation to our God which sitteth upon the throne, and unto the Lamb. . . . These are they which came out of the great tribulation (Rev. 7:9, 14b).

The Holy Spirit, though withdrawn in a special way at the rapture of the Church, will nevertheless have a ministry in the world during the tribulation much the same as He had in Old Testament times.

This is not purported to be a complete list of the characteristics of the tribulation, but it in general describes the nature of the tribulation.

The relation of the Church to the tribulation. It has already been made clear that the belief of the author is that the Church will not go through the tribulation. Christ will meet His Church in the air before the seventieth week of Daniel or the tribulation begins, and the Church will be with Him in heaven until they both return together at His Second Coming after the tribulation. During this time the Church will be judged (2 Cor. 5:10), rewarded (1 Cor. 3:14), and married (Rev. 19:7-9). Some premillennialists believe that the rapture of the Church will occur either in the middle of the tribulation or at the end of it. It is not necessary to go into all the arguments for each of these views, for premillennialism as a system is not dependent on one's view of the rapture. However, for the sake of com-

pleteness some reasons will be mentioned why the pretribula-
tion rapture view is the most consistent one.

(1) If the Church is a mystery, as has been shown, she must
be removed before the tribulation, for the tribulation is not a
mystery but was the subject of Old Testament revelation.

(2) If the restrainer, the Holy Spirit, is to be removed
before the tribulation (2 Thess. 2:1-10) then the Church also
must be taken out of the world.

(3) The promise of Revelation 3:10 is that the whole
Church will be taken away before the hour of temptation begins. This does not mean that she will be kept through the
trial, for as Thiessen observes, "when it would have been so
easy to write ἐν τῇ ὥρα, if the writer had meant preservation
in that hour, why should he write ἐκ τῆς ὥρας as he did?" [3]

(4) If the church had no part in the first sixty-nine weeks of
Daniel's prophecy, how can it be a part of the future seventieth week?

(5) The twenty-four elders, which picture the Church, are
seen in heaven before the tribulation begins. That they represent the Church is seen from their own declaration that they
represent a crowned throng that is there only through the
virtue of the redeeming blood of Christ.

(6) The exhortations concerning the rapture indicate that
the Church will not go through the tribulation. The rapture is
called a comforting hope (1 Thess. 4:18); a purifying hope
(1 John 3:3); and a blessed hope (Tit. 2:13). None of these
would be true if the church had seven years in which to prepare
to meet her Lord. In addition, believers are told to look (Tit.

[3] *Bibliotheca Sacra*, XCII, 203.

2:13), watch (1 Thess. 5:6), and wait (1 Cor. 3:7) for their Saviour.

All the evidence points to the fact that the rapture will occur before the tribulation. Let it be said again that one's attitude toward the tribulation or the rapture is not a decisive factor in premillennialism.

The end of the tribulation. Feinberg has given a good summary of the important events which will occur at the end of the tribulation which summary is included that the picture might be complete.

> First of all, Israel is regathered from all the ends of the earth whither they have been scattered. They are judged by the Lord in the wilderness according to the prophecy of Ezekiel, and restored in blessing to their own land, there to be a blessing to all the nations of the earth. Second, many Gentiles are saved out of the Great Tribulation. . . . Third, Satan is conquered and bound and consigned to the bottomless pit. Fourth, the beast and the false prophet are cast into the lake of fire. Fifth, the battle of Armageddon marks the end of all war on earth. . . . Sixth, Christ Jesus . . . comes in visible glory with His angels . . . as KING OF KINGS AND LORD OF LORDS. Finally, when He sits on the throne of His glory, the nations are brought before Him to be judged as to the treatment of His brethren, the remnant of Israel during the Great Tribulation.[4]

II. THE MILLENNIUM

The millennium is the period of a thousand years of the visible, earthly reign of the Lord Jesus Christ, who, after His return from heaven, will fulfill during that period the promises

[4] *Op. cit.,* pp. 135-36.

contained in the Abrahamic, Davidic, and new covenants to Israel, will bring the whole world to a knowledge of God, and will lift the curse from the whole creation.

Its literal character. That the millennium is a literal period of time is practically only a conclusion of all that has been said before. The question of literal interpretation has been discussed at length. The last book of the Bible, which is an unveiling, not a veiling, plainly teaches that there will be a kingdom rule of Christ on earth for a thousand years (Rev. 20). Let the amillennialist notice carefully that this is the first mention in this entire book of this chapter which has been called the keystone of premillennialism. This passage must be taken as literally as the rest of Scripture. Alford, the great Greek scholar, rightly says:

> I cannot consent to distort words from their plain sense and chronological place in the prophecy, on account of any risk of abuses which the doctrine of the millennium may bring with it. Those who lived next to the Apostles, and the whole Church for 300 years, understood them in the plain literal sense: and it is a strange sight in these days to see expositors who are among the first in reverence of antiquity, complacently casting aside the most cogent instance of consensus which primitive antiquity presents. As regards the text itself, no legitimate treatment of it will extort what is known as the spiritual interpretation now in fashion.[5]

The literal millennium is made necessary, then, not merely by one passage in the Revelation, but by all that has been cited before by way of Scriptural evidence for the kingdom age. Revelation 20 simply gives the duration of that period.

Its importance. A literal millennium is the natural result of

[5] *The Greek Testament,* IV, 732.

all that has been said concerning literal interpretation, the fulfillment of the Abrahamic, Davidic, and new covenants. When the millennium is spiritualized, then these promises of the Word of God must also be spiritualized.

Its designations. The millennium is called by different descriptive titles in the Scriptures, and these will be listed without comment. It is called the kingdom of heaven (in real form, Matt. 6:10); the kingdom of God (in real form, Luke 19:11); the kingdom of Christ (Rev. 11:15); the regeneration (Matt. 19:28); the times of restitution (Acts 3:18-24); the times of refreshing (Acts 3:19); the fulness of times (Eph. 1:10); and the world to come (Heb. 2:5).

Its earthly character. The kingdom will be established on the earth.

> They shall not hurt nor destroy in all my holy mountain: for the earth shall be full of the knowledge of the Lord, as the waters cover the sea (Isa. 11:9).

> And the Lord shall be king over all the earth: in that day shall there be one Lord, and his name one (Zech. 14:9). (*Cf.* Psa. 2:8; Isa. 42:4; Jer. 23:5; Dan. 2:35, 44, 45; 7:24-27; Lk. 1:31-33)

There will be certain physical changes in the earth during the millennium. There will be a cleavage in the Mount of Olives when Christ comes:

> And his feet shall stand in that day upon the mount of Olives, which is before Jerusalem on the east, and the mount of Olives shall cleave in the midst thereof toward the east and toward the west, and there shall be a very great valley; and half of the mountain shall remove toward the north, and half of it toward the south (Zech. 14:4, *cf.* Matt. 24:3; Acts 1:11-12).

There will be a river of living water flowing from Jerusalem, which statement may be taken literally:

> And it shall be in that day that living waters shall go out from Jerusalem; half of them toward the former sea, and half of them toward the hinder sea: in summer and winter shall it be (Zech. 14:8, *cf.* Ezek. 47:1; Joel 3:18).

Jerusalem will be exalted (Zech. 14:10), and there is no reason to doubt but that this will be literal and that the city by means of certain physical changes shall be exalted above the surrounding hills. In addition there will be longevity of life during the millennium, for "the child shall die an hundred years old" (Isa. 65:20; *cf.* Psa. 90:10). Furthermore, animal nature will be radically changed, for "they shall not hurt nor destroy in all my holy mountain, saith the Lord" (Isa. 65:25; *cf.* Isa. 11:6-9; Hosea 2:18). The whole of nature will be newly productive:

> The wilderness and the solitary place shall be glad for them; and the desert shall rejoice, and blossom as the rose. . . . Then shall the lame man leap as an hart, and the tongue of the dumb sing: for in the wilderness shall waters break out, and streams in the desert. And the parched ground shall become a pool, and the thirsty land springs of water: in the habitation of dragons, where each lay, shall be grass with reeds and rushes (Isa. 35:1, 6, 7; *cf.* 41:17-20; 55:12-13; Rom. 8:22 ff.).

The kingdom, as promised, will be on the earth, though the earth will be changed in the ways that have been named.

Its government. The Head of the government in the millennium is the King, Christ Jesus.

> Behold, the days come, saith the Lord, that I will raise unto
> David a righteous Branch, and a King shall reign and prosper,
> and shall execute judgment and justice in the earth (Jer. 23:5;
> *cf.* Lk. 1:31-33; Rev. 11:15; 19:6).

Concerning the character of Christ's reign, the Scriptures teach
that it will be in the plenitude of the Spirit (Isa. 11:2-5), that
it will be in equity and justice (Jer. 23:5-6), that sin will be
punished (Psa. 2:9; 72:1-4; Isa. 65:20; Zech. 14:16-21),
that it will be prosperous and glorious (Jer. 23:5; Isa. 24:23),
and that it will be a reign of peace (Isa. 2:4; 11:5-9; 65:25;
Mic. 4:3).

The center of government in the millennium will be Jerusalem. "For out of Zion shall go forth the law, and the word of
the Lord from Jerusalem" (Isa. 2:3). Even Hamilton admits
that if interpreted literally the Scripture teaches this fact.[6]
Jerusalem will be a holy place (Isa. 4:3-5); a place of great
glory (Isa. 24:23); the site of the future temple (Isa. 33:20);
a praise in the earth (Isa. 62:1-7); rebuilt (Jer. 31:38-40); the
spiritual center for the whole earth (Zech. 8:20-23); the city
to which Christ returns (Zech 14:4); and the joy of the whole
earth (Psa. 48:2).

Three groups of people will be related to the millennial government. Israel, regathered and turned to the Lord in salvation,
will be exalted, blessed, and favored throughout the period.
Sufficient has already been said about this. The nations will be
subjects of the King during the millennium. "Yea, all kings
shall fall down before him: all nations shall serve him" (Psa.
72:11; *cf.* 86:9; Dan. 7:13-14; Mic. 4:2; Zech. 8:22). In
addition, the Church will reign with Christ, not as a subject

[6] *Op. cit.*, p. 46.

of the King, but as one who rightfully shares the rule (2 Tim. 2:12; Rev. 5:10; 20:6).

Its spiritual character. There are three questions which are related to this problem. First, there is the question of the unsaved in the millennium. It seems clear from Isaiah 65:20, Zechariah 14:16-18, and Revelation 20:7-8 that there will be unsaved people in the millennium. Involved in this question is the judgment of the nations (Matt. 25:31-46), for if the judgment is individual, then it seems that no unredeemed person will enter the kingdom age; but if the judgment is of national groups, then conceivably some unsaved people will enter the kingdom. However, there is no evidence that those who enter the kingdom as a result of this judgment will have redeemed bodies so that children may be born during the millennial period who may or may not come to a personal saving knowledge of the Lord. In any case anyone who is saved will be saved by the blood of Christ, for that is the only way that anyone in any age can be saved (Zech. 13:1). Obviously, this question does not make or break the entire premillennial system.

Secondly, there is the question of Christian ordinances in the millennium. Again, this is not a determining question, but it seems to follow from the distinctive character of the Church in this age that Christian ordinances will be terminated at the beginning of the millennium. The Lord Himself placed the terminus of the great commission as the end of the age (Matt. 28:20), and it seems as though the making and baptizing of disciples will also terminate then. The Lord's Supper also was to be observed "till He come" (1 Cor. 11:26) and will not be observed during the millennium.

Thirdly, there is the more difficult question of the offerings in the millennium. This is always seized upon by amillennialists as manifesting an irreparable weakness in the premillennial system. It involves these Scripture passages: Ezekiel 43:18-46:24; Zechariah 14:16; and Hebrews 10:4, 14. The Ezekiel passage is usually interpreted in one of three ways: (1) the description is of the actual temple that was built in history by the remnant when they returned from Babylon; (2) the description is symbolic of the Christian church; (3) the temple is yet to be built and the sacrificial system reestablished during the millennium.

Basically, the question is one of literal versus allegorical interpretation. If literal interpretation is accepted, only the third view is possible; therefore, it must be accepted if we are going to be consistent with the principles of interpretation set forth herein. It is admitted that the question is not an easy one, but it is not one on which the entire premillennial system either stands or falls. Viewed in proper perspective it is merely a detail of the kingdom age. The existence or nonexistence of the kingdom itself certainly does not depend on the question of offerings.

The issue also involves the question of whether or not the temple will be rebuilt. The plain sense of the chapters in Ezekiel teach that it will be rebuilt, and this New Testament verse seems to clinch the argument:

> Who opposeth and exalteth himself above all that is called God, or that is worshipped; so that he as God sitteth in the temple of God, shewing himself that he is God (2 Thess. 2:4).

This verse teaches that during the tribulation period the temple will be in existence, and that sacrifices will be offered there

(Dan. 9:27). Therefore, the temple will be there, but will offerings be continued after Christ returns and is personally reigning? Premillennialists in general answer in the affirmative. We agree with this, but, in order to keep the discussion within proper bounds, will only defend this against the most commonly urged arguments against literal offerings in the millennium.

The first argument against literal sacrifices is that the dimensions of the temple as given by Ezekiel are far too large to fit into the topography of the land. This is easily answered by referring to the physical changes in the land which will occur during the millennium (Zech. 14:4-5; Isa. 29:6). These will allow for the literal temple, and:

> If there is going to be such a temple, and we believe that there is, what would be the use and purpose of the same if it were not to be used for worship and that worship to be conducted in the manner as explained by Ezekiel in the same passage? That would be by animal sacrifices.[7]

The second objection often raised is that such offerings would be a retrogression in the program of God, according to Hebrews 9 and 10 which teach that sacrifices came to an end with Christ's death. Mitchell gives a sane answer to this question which, though lengthy, is quoted in full:

> To answer this objection, let us step back and look at God's entire program from a distance. Throughout the Old Testament, the Jews were worshiping God in their tabernacle and temple through animal sacrifices. They were looking forward to a day of peace and prosperity, a kingdom over which their Messiah would be their King. Their Messiah came, but they refused to accept Him as such and continued with their sacrifices. In the meantime, He was crucified as the one great Sacrifice sufficient

[7] John L. Mitchell, *Animal Sacrifices in the Millennium*, p. 42.

for all. Outside of the small circle of believers of that day, this meant nothing to the vast majority except that an imposter had been put to death.

Now then, the Epistle to the Hebrews was written not to the Jewish people in general, but especially to them who had professed faith in Christ as the one great and final Sacrifice but since then had either continued in or gone back to their animal sacrifices. . . . They were warned not to return to their sacrifices since Christ had set them free. The context is concerning animal sacrifices during the day of grace. The subject before us is that of animal sacrifices in the millennium day.

The Church will be taken out of the earth at the rapture at which time God's program for the Jew will be resumed and continue from where it was at the time of Christ's death. . . . [The millennium] will simply be a continuation of the old order, this time with Christ accepted as and reigning as King. The Jews will continue their animal sacrifices in worship as they did before Christ died. It is true that these sacrifices will be types and symbols of their faith in Christ's death, but that does not make them nonetheless real. There will probably be mingled sorrow and joy in these sacrifices as they recall how their fathers refused to accept this Christ as their Messiah and how now they have the privilege of seeing it all so clearly.[8]

We conclude, then, that animal sacrifices will be offered in the millennium.

Its end. At the end of the millennium certain events take place. First, Satan will be loosed for a little season, and he will attempt a last revolt (Rev. 20:7-10). This will demonstrate that even the very best environment in the world will not change the corruptness of the unregenerated heart. Satan will then meet his final doom by being cast into the lake of fire (Rev. 20:10). After this a stupendous event about which there is little revealed will occur—the passing away of the present heaven and earth (Isa. 65:17; 66:22; Heb. 1:10-12; 2 Pet.

[8] *Ibid.,* pp. 43-44.

3:3-13; Rev. 20:11; 21:1). Next follows the resurrection and judgment at the great white throne of all the unsaved dead and their commitment to the lake of fire forever (Rev. 20:12-15; 21:8; 22:10-15). The final work of God is the creation of the new heaven and the new earth (Rev. 21:1) and the ushering in of the eternal state.

A final word is necessary concerning the duration of Christ's reign. It has seemed incongruous to some that the reign of Christ is referred to as a thousand years and as eternal. One passage—1 Corinthians 15:24-28—seems to teach that Christ yields up the kingdom at the end of the millennium, but Chafer rightly points out that:

> The statement is meant to signify that, when all is subdued and divine authority is restored in full, the Son, who has ruled by the authority of the Father throughout the thousand years and has put down all enemies, will go on ruling under that same authority of the Father's as subject as ever to the First Person. This more clarified meaning of the text removes the suggestion of conflict between an everlasting reign and a supposed limited reign of Christ. He will, as so fully assured elsewhere, reign on the throne of David forever.[9]

This concludes the relation of premillennialism to eschatology. Premillennialism is the only system which presents an eschatology consistent with the principles of interpretation and the plain teaching of the Word of God. We have dealt with some eschatological problems and tried to indicate the solutions, but because in the over-all picture they are not major problems, premillennialism, in eschatology, rests on a solid basis.

[9] *Op. cit.,* V, 374.

Chapter 9

Conclusion

The purpose of this book has been to examine in a positive way the basis of the premillennial faith. Of necessity, reference has been made to opponents' claims as they challenged the very basis on which premillennialism rests, but in general the aim was not critical or negative. All the details of prophecy were not examined, nor was it claimed that premillennialists agree on every detail. But disagreement on details does not constitute a major problem to the system as a whole, and while many of these problems were discussed and solutions which seemed most consistent to the premillennial system were offered, it is evident that they do not affect the basis of the faith.

We have traced the history of premillennialism giving special emphasis to the subapostolic age. It was clearly shown that the premillennial faith is not a modern invention. From the study of the principles of interpretation it was demonstrated that premillennialism alone is consistent with the principle of literal interpretation as it extends to all fields of Biblical interpretation including eschatology. Literal interpretation is the only safe method of interpretation, and on this principle premillennialism rests.

The main burden of the work was the relation of the Abrahamic, Davidic, and new covenants to premillennialism. The

main question resolved itself to this: will the unfulfilled provisions of these covenants be fulfilled? In answering this it was
necessary to examine one particular New Testament problem
under each covenant. Under the Abrahamic covenant the
Church and Israel were carefully distinguished proving that
the Church does not fulfill the yet unfulfilled provisions of that
covenant. Under the Davidic covenant the problem of the New
Testament teaching concerning the kingdom was discussed,
including the offer, postponement, and future fulfillment of
the kingdom promises. That the kingdom is now in mystery form
is one of the major proofs that the promises to David have not
been abrogated. Further, the New Testament clearly teaches
that Israel will yet fulfill the promises of the new covenant
during the millennium. Thus, premillennialism is the only system of interpretation which can properly make place for the
covenants of God.

Certain aspects of the doctrine of ecclesiology were discussed,
chiefly the distinctiveness of the Church as the body of saints
in this age only. This means that there is no overlapping on
either side of the age of God's program for His people Israel.
The teachings of eschatology were merely a natural result of
all that had been said before. The space devoted to this chapter
should show that premillennialism is far more than a system
of eschatology.

Each of these factors—the historical evidence, the science of
hermeneutics, the Abrahamic covenant, the Davidic covenant,
the new covenant, the teachings of ecclesiology, and the teachings of eschatology—is like a plank in the platform of premillennialism. Altogether they form an harmonious whole and

an unshakeable basis upon which premillennialism rests. And underlying it all is the very nature of God Himself in that what He has plainly spoken He will do, and what He has assuredly promised He will perform. This is the basis of the premillennial faith.

INDEX OF SCRIPTURE TEXTS

158